FORGIVE ME, I'M HUMAN

FORGIVE ME, I'M HUMAN

by
CARL H. STEVENS, JR.

New Leaf Press

First Printing: March, 1991
Second Printing: May, 1991

Library of Congress Catalog Number: 90-64351
ISBN: 0-89221-192-X

Cover art by: Drew and Karen Janssen

Typesetting by: Total Type & Graphics
                  Berryville, AR

Contents

Introduction

At the signing of the Declaration of Independence, Benjamin Franklin told the delegates to the convention, "We must all hang together, or assuredly we shall all hang separately"! The task before us as believers is a great one. We need every available hand on the plow. It is no time for turning to the left or to the right—our focus, as the Church, must be upon our Head, Jesus Christ. His Word needs to be proclaimed like never before. His hymns and praises need to be sung as loudly as they ever have been sung if the sweet sound of His amazing grace is to reach the ears of those who are wretched without Him. And it must reach believers who feel wretched because of their failure and guilt.

David wrote in Psalm 41:1, "Blessed is he that considereth the poor: the Lord will deliver him in time of trouble." Poverty is more than simply a lack of money. The Hebrew word refers to something hanging or swinging like a door. Picture those who are lost without Christ. Those who have never received Him are swinging between heaven and hell, hanging between an eternity of joy and one of torment. Their destinies hinge upon what we, as Christians, do with what we have received. Will we gather in the poor by going forward in unity and spreading the good news of Christ, or will we scatter them as we fight and accuse each other?

Consider another kind of poverty—believers who have fallen. Sin has impoverished them spiritually. Their power has been diminished. We cannot turn away from the poor and the feeble in the Church. "Therefore, strengthen the hands that are weak and the knees that are feeble" (Hebrews 12:12; NASB). There is a great need today for genuine edification within the church of Jesus Christ.

The eternal redemption we have received through Christ's finished work on the cross is our common bond. Regardless of our denominational preference, we have been accepted in the Beloved by the blood of the Lamb. The fields are ripe, ready for harvesting those in need of compassion, reconciliation, and restoration. In the parable of the Good Samaritan, a man was beaten, robbed, and left for dead. Neither the priest nor the Levite found time to help this man in his hour of need. They did not even want to be found on the same side of the road with him! Maybe they were on the way to fulfill a religious rite or make a sacrifice. "To obey is better than sacrifice" (1 Sam. 15:22). Will we live to fulfill our religious norms, or will we fulfill Christ's commission and reach down to share God's love, mercy, and grace?

In the early 1970s, a number of young adults joined our church. Some of them had extremely long hair and dressed in what appeared to be rags. In spite of their appearance, the majority of them sincerely wanted to follow Jesus and learn His Word. They made mistakes. Some found it difficult to break long-standing habits. We, the leaders of the church, could have robbed these young Christians of the joy of walking with Christ by imposing man-made standards of behavior on them. But their wounds needed to be bound, not exposed. We ministered to them and many went on to Bible school. Several are now full time pastors and missionaries. Through compassion and investment, we helped them go forward with God. What has been the result? Many souls have been led to Christ and multiple nations reached through their fruitful lives. A lasting capacity for excellence came as a result of holding up a true picture of the grace of God.

The Lord of Zephaniah 3:17 rests in His love. "Rest" means to stand silent and still. As Satan—the accuser of the brethren described in Revelation 12:10—makes his indictments, God remains immovable in His love. The sin issue has been settled and His justice has been satisfied. God answered the devil's accusations once and for all at Calvary. "They overcame him by the blood of the Lamb" (Rev. 12:11). Christ's blood bought our positional standing in Him, and His Word supplies us with the power to experience that standing. Jesus paid it all. Satan's chief aim in his attack against the Church is to distract our minds from this simple truth. If the owner of a perfectly operational automobile believes it is broken, he won't drive it. Christ sits at God's right hand with abundant power; but the vehicle remains inactive because of believing a lie! This is Satan's strategy.

The Psalmist said, "My soul cleaveth unto the dust: quicken Thou me according to Thy Word." Apart from our position in Christ and His Word in us, we can only respond to situations according to what we are, which is dust. Instead of kicking up the dust, today is a time for Christians to "stand still, and see the salvation of the Lord" (Ex. 14:13-14). The world, like the Egyptian army of old, is closing in on the Church. Let us not murmur, complain, or fight among ourselves. His rest is glorious (Isa. 11:10). As we come to Him with our labors and burdens, He will give us rest. He is at the right hand of God and we are in Him. We can serve Him with confidence and power, knowing that there is not a single thing that can separate us from that love.

—C.H.S.

Let others sing to the hero who wins in the
    ceaseless fray,
Who, over the crushed and fallen, pursueth
    his upward way;
For him let them weave the laurel, to him
    be their paean sung,
Whom the kindly fates have chosen, who
    are happy their loved among;
But mine be a different message, some
    soul in its stress to reach;
To bind, o'er the wound of failure, the
    balm of pitying speech;
To whisper: "Be up and doing, for courage
    at last prevails"
I sing—who have supped with Failure,—
    I sing to the man who fails."
        —Alfred J. Waterhouse

ONE

FAILURE IS A FACT OF LIFE

Failure is as much a part of the human experience as breathing. Needless to say, no one is perfect. Babe Ruth, the great home run hitter for the New York Yankees in the 1920s and 30s, holds a spot in baseball history for slamming 714 balls out of the park. However, what you might not know is that he also struck out 1,330 times. For every glorious triumph at the plate, he had two miserable failures.

General Douglas McArthur, fleeing the Philippines in apparent failure, made that legendary pronouncement: "I shall return!" He did return in one of the greatest morale-boosting war efforts in the Pacific.

John Mark quit the first missionary team sent out in the Book of Acts. But church history records that he later became Peter's right hand man, authored one of the four Gospels, was the first bishop of Alexandria, and died as a martyr for the faith. Failure for him was not the end, but only the beginning.

The Bible: A History of Failures

Human history began with failure. Adam and Eve failed to keep the one simple commandment given to them. When the flooded world emerged from judgment, Noah, the one man who had found grace in the eyes of the Lord, planted a vineyard and got drunk. Abraham, the father of our faith, was faithless when it came to his beautiful wife. Twice he lied about his relationship with her in order to save his own skin. He could not trust God for the timing of the promised seed. Instead, he listened to Sarah and fathered Ishmael by Hagar, her Egyptian maid. David, the king after God's own heart, committed adultery and murder following a tragic decision not to go to battle. Peter, the pillar of the church, professed his readiness to follow Christ even if it meant prison or death. The very next few verses of Scripture record his failure under pressure. Both Moses, in the Old Testament, and Paul, in the New, were men who were responsible for bloodshed due to their misguided attempts to serve God.

Failure is the underside of human existence, the unlovely part that everyone wants to hide. The Bible records the failures of these "greats" to give us a realistic picture of man's condition and God's merciful nature. Long before the press rallied to "tell all" by exposé, God's Word was faithful to give the whole story. The Apostle Paul cried out in painful honesty, "in my flesh dwells no good thing!" David, the sweet psalmist of Israel wept, "I was shapen in iniquity and in sin did my mother conceive me." Any approach to Christianity which does not include failure is ridiculous and unscriptural. All the foundational doctrines of faith—atonement, saving grace, justification by faith—all presuppose human failure.

The Anatomy of a Hero

What makes a hero? What are the guts of a human success story? James 5:17 encourages our hearts by using Elijah as an example in prayer. He was a man "subject to like passions as we are." Elijah was in a paranoid, depressed state bordering on suicide in 1 Kings 19, yet he is our "hero," inspiring us to believe God beyond our own frailties. The very character flaws which surfaced when he was in the pressure cooker of warfare make us identify with his battles and victories. When we read that he persevered in prayer until he saw the cloud the size of a man's hand, we are inspired to pray until the nail-scarred Hand becomes visible in our circumstances, too. (See 1 Kings 18:42-45)

"Like... as we are." Glorious words! Raymond Lull, early missionary to the Muslims, set up training centers for Muslim evangelism and sent out evangelists. Then he received the call to personally go. At the last minute, even as crowds of well-wishers thronged the docks, Lull panicked at the thought of Muslim torture and martyrdom. He unloaded the ship and refused to go. Shortly thereafter, having mastered his fears, he went out on a later ship. Lull successfully evangelized Muslims for years and was an eager martyr for the faith at age eighty-three in Tunisia. "Like... as we are!"

Dwight L. Moody, elder statesman of the faith, had lapses when his old temper broke out. Once, just after an evangelistic meeting as he was urging men to give their hearts in prayer to Christ, a man approached him and grossly insulted him. Instantly, Mr. Moody thrust the man from him, sending him reeling down a flight of stairs. Mr. Moody immediately recovered himself and apologized before everyone. He was "like... as we are."

St. Augustine, ex-playboy of his age, fought a continual battle against his former temptations; John Wesley had a terrible marriage; Charles Spurgeon, a successful pastor, smoked until shamed by a tobacco advertisement which used his name; then he quit. They were "like... as we are."

Who are the real heros? The unlikely models of perfection or the men and women who battled the flesh and beat the odds? In the long list of faith heros of Hebrews, chapter eleven, there are only one or two whose faults are not recorded in earlier chapters of the Bible. They are examples of faith, not infallibility.

TWO

THE NATURE OF THE BEAST

There is so much good in the worst of us
And so much bad in the best of us
That it hardly becomes any of us
To talk about the rest of us.[1]

What does it mean to be human? "I am fearfully and wonderfully made!" the Psalmist exclaimed, echoing the self-conscious response of every soul. "God said, let us make man in our image, after our likeness: and let them have dominion" (Gen. 1:26). But when man's free volition was used to turn from God in Genesis, all of humanity was plunged into the darkness of sin. Adam's original sin condemned the entire human race. "Through one man sin entered into the world, and death through sin, and so death spread to all men, because all sinned" (Rom. 5:12 NASB).

How ludicrous it is to compare or measure the

production of what comes out of Adam! "We are all as an unclean thing, and all our righteousnesses are as filthy rags" (Isa. 64:6). "Every man at his best state is altogether vanity!" (Ps. 39:5). "There is none righteous, no, not one" (Rom. 3:10). God has included all of us in Adam's unrighteousness that He might extend His mercy to all in the gift of Jesus Christ. It does not matter how few or how many our transgressions have been; it all needs to be forgiven and cleansed by Christ's payment on the cross.

" 'Lord, how oft shall my brother sin against me, and I forgive him? Till seven times?' Jesus answered Peter, 'I say not unto thee seven times, but until seventy times seven!' " Jesus illustrated the principle of forgiveness with this story:

"A king wanted to settle accounts with his servants. As he began, a man who owed him ten thousand talents was brought to him. Since he was not able to pay, the master ordered that he and his wife and his children and all that he had be sold to repay the debt. The servant fell on his knees before him. 'Be patient with me', he begged, 'and I will pay back everything.' The servant's master took pity on him, cancelled the debt and let him go. But, when that servant went out, he found one of his fellow servants who owed him a hundred denari. He grabbed him and began to choke him. 'Pay back what you owe me!' he demanded. His fellowservant fell to his knees and begged him, 'Be patient with me, and I will pay you back.' But he refused. Instead, he went off and had the man thrown into prison until he could pay the debt. When the other servants saw what had happened, they were greatly distressed and went and told their master everything that had happened. Then the master called the servant in.

'You wicked servant', he said, 'I cancelled all that debt of yours because you begged me to. Shouldn't you have had mercy on your fellowservant just as I had on you?' In anger his master turned him over to the jailers to be tortured, until he should pay back all that he owed."

Jesus concluded the story by saying, "This is how My heavenly Father will treat each of you unless you forgive your brother from the heart" (Matt. 18:22-35; NASB).

We are to forgive others as God has forgiven us. This is not a system of works—forgive to be forgiven, but as He forgives us, we forgive others, giving grace for grace through the Holy Spirit. The only people Jesus was ever angry with in the Gospels were the Pharisees, because they distorted the image of God and refused to pass out the forgiveness they had received and had been delegated to give.

There is a Pharisee within each one of us who is a greater sinner than the person who has obviously failed. Many years ago, a lovely Christian woman attended a series of meetings at my church, the topic of which was God's unconditional love. For fifteen years she had been living with a good-for-nothing alcoholic husband. All those years she had carried the financial and emotional load of the family. After hearing about the unconditional love and forgiveness of God, she went home and waited up for her drunken husband. Realizing the bountiful mercy that had been shown to her through Jesus Christ, she was deeply moved with love toward him. He arrived home at three that morning and collapsed in a drunken stupor on the living room couch. She knelt and prayed. When he awoke hours later, she served him coffee and waited for him to sit up. "Forgive me for not loving you these fifteen years," she said. "I have lived in reaction to you. Will you forgive me?" He was so touched by her change of attitude that he began attending the meetings, too. He gave his heart to Christ and has been faithfully serving Him now for over twenty years!

One sin, alone, dooms the sinner to an eternity in hell; and that is Adam's sin, committed before any of us were ever born. We have no right to withhold the forgiveness that has been extended to all, however many or few their trespasses have been. God's forgiveness is all-encompassing and final.

> If ye forgive men their trespasses, your heavenly Father will also forgive you: but if ye forgive not men their trespasses, neither will your Father forgive your trespasses (Matt. 6:14-15).

If we refuse to give the grace we have received, our experience will be a difficult one. We automatically come under the law by which we evaluate others. Under the law of sin and death, we were made sinners. As recipients of the law of the Spirit of life in Christ, we are made righteous. There is nothing to boast in or require of others. No one is any good in themselves, but everyone is wonderful in Christ!

Forgiveness magnifies the Forgiver instead of the failure. Lewis Sperry Chafer says that no demonstration of grace is possible unless there are objects of grace, and there could be no objects of grace apart from the presence and experience of sin.[2] The fall of man did not stop the plan or purpose of God which was to create man for His glory. Our need magnifies God's goodness which was demonstrated on an old rugged cross. Forgiveness which covers all accounts glorifies His nature of grace.

Man's Intrinsic Emptiness

Adam's sin was imputed to every human being, and the adamic sin nature was imparted genetically to every member of the human race. Even before a soul is conscious of sin, it sins. Within man's complex awareness is the consciousness of God, conscience of what is right, and self-consciousness of falling short of the ideals of perfection.

To magnify the chasm between man's original state and his experiential condition, God gave the Law. Even as Moses was receiving the Law, the people were breaking it. They sinned as they waited for their sin to be defined. Before Moses had reached the bottom of Mt. Sinai with the slabs of stone, they were riotously transgressing the first commandment "Thou shalt have no other gods before Me" as they danced around the golden calf.

The Law of Moses activates man's conscience which activates the will which activates the energy of the flesh which can only sin. The Law intensifies the self-awareness and activity of sin. "For I would not have known about coveting if the Law had not said, 'You shall not covet.' But sin, taking opportunity through the commandment, produced in me coveting of every kind; for apart from the Law, sin is dead ... but when the commandment came, sin became alive, and I died" (Rom. 7:7-9; NASB). The apostle Paul knew that the Law was good and right but it only made him realize how carnal and sinful he was. He found himself in a struggle of wanting to please God and yet being unable to.

Man, created at a point of time in innocence and having chosen to live apart from God, became destined to live forever in the hell of wasted potential. The capacity of the subjective mind is such that the child who lies at age three never recovers from the effects of that lie though the conscious mind may not remember it the next day. The soul's computer indelibly records every decision and every event. In desperation, man turns to religion in an effort to purge the conscience of its record of failure and to assuage the consciousness of a dissatisfied Maker. Knowledge of good and knowledge of evil vie within the self-essence giving conflicting messages to the conscience, self-consciousness, perception, logic, and volition. The emotions become poisoned as the objective mind is overrun by the subjective signals. The lack of conscious definition creates a condition of fear. Every phobia traces back to this process of the fallen psyche. No psychiatrist can take the mind back far enough to get rid of all the roots of guilt because they originate from a pre-natal cause!

Though one may be privileged to grow up in a good family which honors the principles of morality and is disciplined to do good, the sickness of the inner condition cannot be eradicated. Education, counsel, and religion can only lessen the blow of how much the individual will reap in his fallen state. Man buries himself in his work, his hobbies, his talents; he uses relationships, responsibilities, physical opiates, and stimulants to alleviate the oppressive reality of being a worm! He educates his mind and trains his responses, but deeply rooted within is the consciousness of God's verdict.

> The whole head is sick, and the whole heart is faint. From the sole of the foot even to the head there is nothing sound in it, only bruises, welts, and raw wounds, not pressed out or bandaged, nor softened with oil (Isa. 1:5-6; NASB).

The diagnosis of a fallen nation perfectly describes the state of man in his fallen condition. Though he may try to do, give and be, when it is all said and done, in the hours of darkness and quiet the heart cries out in emptiness, "I cannot change me!"

The dominating need to be inwardly filled drives man to attach himself to an infinite number of objects as this eternal capacity to receive from God becomes transferred to temporal targets which can never fully satisfy. Because man's needs are always increasing, new objects must be continually found and exploited. This chain of bondage is only broken by becoming filled with the object of our original design: God, himself. Christ identified with our spiritual emptiness when He died in our place to satisfy the judicial demands of a broken law. When bona fide need becomes attached to Calvary's love, then forgiveness, justification, communion, and fellowship fill the human heart. The devastating effects of the fall are neutralized and the insatiable cycle of sin and death is broken.

Man was created to enjoy an exchanged life. Adam (the old sin nature) holds onto his life in self-preservation through a myriad of security systems, but Christ offers death to the old man via the Cross to rid us of the very source of insecurity and emptiness. The Christian must be continually saved from the self-life by being constantly filled through a faith appropriation process.

The moment the soul is not being actively filled with God's Spirit, a spiritual vacuum is created. Just because Christians do not commit sin, they think they are spiritual. Overt sin is simply the expression of a soul that has been living outside of vital fellowship with Christ. We can live in the carnality of an empty mind a long time before evil becomes apparent. The measure in which the soul does not have a living relationship with Christ and His Word through grace will be the measure that it will need the world and natural relationships to sustain it, though these "fillers" may not appear to be overtly sinful.

Although God is not the author of evil or the minister of sin, when a Christian lives for an extended period of time in this condition, he may actually need a dramatic fall to wake him up to his inwardly deprived state. The mind so subtly reverts to that tree of knowledge which feeds the old rationale! Everything we do has its source in spiritual life or spiritual death. Either the head is Christ or the head is spiritually sick. Living outside of communion and dependence upon Christ is to be cut off from the experience of His life. We are either living in Christ or in our knowledge about Him. This is the difference between a relationship and religion. Either we are experiencing what we have been made in Christ, or what we have been made in Adam. Morality, works, religion, and reform seem right but leave us in the dilemma of Adam's impotence. "Received ye the Spirit by the works of the Law, or by the hearing of faith? Are ye so foolish? having begun in the Spirit, are ye now made perfect by the flesh?" (Gal. 3:2-3).

One degree off from grace makes the mind spiritually sick. "For to be carnally minded is death; but to be spiritually minded is life and peace" (Rom. 8:6). We are always thinking in one of these two standards: self-righteousness or the gift of righteousness through Christ. Holiness does not mean the eradication of sin or the possibility of earthly perfection but, because One died, we are to consider ourselves as dead. We are no longer to be preoccupied with varying degrees of good and evil, but with the God of eternity who has condescended to live in our hearts!

To depart from evil means to depart from a satanic government of thinking which began at the fall through the knowledge of good and evil. Only faith pleases God. We do not try to rid ourselves of what Christ has already taken. That would be unbelief! In Adam, I always fall because Adam is a failure; but in Christ, I can do nothing less than triumph!

Law Strengthens Sin

The Christian lives in a paradox. He stands holy and without blame in God's love and in his position in Christ, but he cannot say that he has no sin. We are seated with Christ at God's right hand, but we do not see all things put under our feet, yet. Old habits, unresolved conflicts, and the ability to sin may still haunt our lives, but we must not be drawn back into an existential struggle with the old creation. The more we react to our state, the greater the power sin will have over us. Paul put it this way: "I find then a law, that, when I would do good, evil is present with me. For I delight in the law of God after the inward man: but I see another law in my members warring against the law of my mind, and bringing me into captivity to the law of sin which is in my members" (Rom. 7:21-23). The strength of sin is in the Law! It is often the legalistic preacher who falls into overt sin. The Law strengthens the power of the flesh because that is what it was designed to do—to magnify man's helplessness.

The poor Christian struggles within the confines of the old nature in an honest effort to conquer it with human goodness. This only prolongs and promotes suffering. As long as we are striving in the battle between good and evil, we are missing the provision of God to altogether escape the realm of the flesh. Fighting evil keeps the soul functioning in the natural temperament where all the problems, wounds, personality disorders, lust patterns, insecurities, frustrations, and pride complexes are. These all have their origin in the old creation. Self cannot cast out self. The oppression of living in self produces the desire for sublimation and, as the corruption that is in the old man is progressive, the human condition worsens. Paul stopped his struggle with sin by reckoning on his co-crucifixion with Christ: "But if I am doing the very thing I do not wish, I am no longer the one doing it, but sin which dwells in me" (Romans 7:20; NASB). His sin had already been judged!

Christ is THE way of thinking that always leads to life! He imparts His nature every time we believe in His specific promises. He warns us not to judge lest we enter back into a former mind-set that has been judged. The law we live by determines the process we experience.

When the believer goes back to his old nature to try to fulfill his new role, it is like trying to put new wine in old wineskins. The Christian can backslide to a state worse than before he was saved because of trying to apply new patches to the worn out garment of his flesh. There is no resolution to the sinfulness of Adam apart from the Cross. No counsel, no prayer, no struggle of the will avails. Sin reigns unto death. Faith in Christ's offering is the only escape. If we refuse our avenue of escape, we are willfully remaining in the cycle of condemnation and syndrome of sin from which Christ died to free us.

Willful Sin

Failing is no longer the issue because Christ took

care of our failures on the cross. Failing grace is now the issue. To stay down after a failure is to fail the grace of God. In Hebrews 10:26, willful sin refers to rejecting the one offering made by Christ which satisfies the justice and holiness of God. Unbelief offers other sacrifices in its place. The effect of faith is rest. When we do not rest in the pure Word of God on the subject of our sins, we continue to try to appease our sense of right.

For the Hebrew Christians, this meant reinstating the Levitical animal sacrifices. For us, it means continuing on in self-effort and its effects of depression, discouragement, guilt, fear, condemnation, judging, and anger from which we have already been delivered. It means being conscious of sins that have been paid for. If we sin, we name it, forsake it, and then forget it because it has already been dealt with at Calvary. When we do not accept the reconciliation Christ died to provide, we continue living as God's enemies expecting His wrath. Treading the blood of the new covenant under one's feet means not accepting its efficacy—saying that it is not enough in itself to make us pleasing to God. To reject God's grace revealed at the Cross is to reject the only means we have of coming into His presence.

The greatest deception in the Church today concerns the grace of God. Grace depends totally on the character and nature of the Giver, not the character and nature of the receiver. "Looking diligently lest any man fail of the grace of God; lest any root of bitterness springing up trouble you, and thereby many be defiled" (Heb. 12:15). The soul must be intensely guarded in this one specific area of grace. Even biblical principles must not be elevated above grace. Every doctrine must come under the government of grace in order to become operationally effective. If we detach a particular truth from grace, we cease to propagate the gospel. Every scriptural precept must remain under the rule of the new covenant. The farther we go from the gospel of grace, the less capacity we will have to experience any of God's characteristics. God cannot operate outside of grace towards us. When we leave the faith race to "deal" with things, we fail the grace that already dealt with them. The soul becomes troubled, alienated, withdrawn, and bitter when it leaves its grace premise. Then it defiles many as the tongue communicates its troubles. Party spirits and taking sides are the inevitable results of failing to magnify Christ.

When we judge, criticize, react, dictate, and legislate to others instead of accepting Christ's shed blood as God's answer for sin, we do despite to the Spirit of grace. Through just one offering are we sanctified and perfected in the eyes of God. The shedding of blood is the only criteria for the remission of sins. To believe that a back-slidden condition can make the saved soul lost is to undervalue the totality of God's provision as well as to misunderstand the very nature of man's condition. God reserves His severest discipline for those who do not take the one offering seriously.

Every holy command from God can be fulfilled only by God's own life. The husband is told to love his wife **exactly** as Christ loves the Church. This is impossible for the natural man who is married to a natural woman! He never will be able to love her with a life that had its beginning in Adam. He will not be able to function as sacrificial lover in his position as Christ's representational head. Eternal life is that life which originates in Christ. It is the only life which returns back to Him. At the Bema Seat Judgment, where believers will receive their rewards, only that which had its origin in Christ's own life will be recognized. Whatever has not gone through identification with Christ's death and has its roots in resurrection ground, belongs to the wood, hay, and stubble of time—the energy of the flesh, emotional impulses, and knowledge without application. Just as Eve was taken out of Adam and then was brought to him, the Church was born out of Christ and will return to Him as His bride. Any fruit she has to present to Him will have been derived from the life that He, himself, gave her. Anything less would be spiritual adultery.

Zerubbabel was to cry "grace, grace" in order for the mountain to be removed. Why? Because it is not by might nor by power, but by God's Spirit that we have the victory. Shout to your failure! Shout to your sin! Shout to guilt and the critical voices of accusation. Grace has overcome every obstacle! The God who brought forth a perfect Son without using Adam's life as intermediary has wrought for himself this great salvation. He seals every believer with His own life in a commitment to live out the life that has been bestowed within.

"I Shall Arise"

There is a wonderful song with a chorus which begins, "Failure isn't final with the Father." Micah, the prophet, was honest about his sin, but he refused to stay defeated in condemnation. "Rejoice not against me O mine enemy," he cried. "When I fall I shall arise!" He knew that there was an end to darkness. Micah could not change the fact of his fall, but he could look up. He knew that his enemies, those who rejoiced at his failure, would live to see him get back up again.

Jack Hyles tells the story of a possessive woman who

wanted her husband to promise her that he would not remarry as her illness brought her close to death. When he could not promise, she refused to die! She rose from her sickbed because she did not want another woman to rejoice over her demise! Micah had that kind of spirit! He knew he would make a comeback. In a world of sin, suffering, unjust persecution, economic uncertainty, and failures of every sort, this is the kind of confident attitude the child of God needs to have.

A son told his mother, "I don't want to go to church today." "You have to go," she replied. "Why?" he asked. She answered, "Because you're forty years old and you're the pastor!" Outward stress and inward discouragement can make anyone want to quit!

King David and his men left the city of Ziklag unguarded when they went off to war only to find total destruction upon their return. Their homes burned to ashes and their loved ones taken captive, to say that they were tempted to be discouraged would be an understatement! The entire army turned on David and wanted to stone him. Anxiety, bitterness, and sorrow incapacitated them all, "but David encouraged himself in the Lord, his God." Even as heaviness was creeping into his emotions, he began to respond to God's grace. He collected himself by reflecting on God's promises. Using the Urim and Thummin, which stand for the Spirit and the Word, he received counsel from above. David did not become introspective or reactionary but in his own way he cried out, "I will arise!"

It is easy to think we are being chastised when we are down. But as spectacles to men and angels, we are given the "down" times to experience and express what we have learned about grace. Who wants to hear our pat

theological answers if we have never gone through any of
the trials which we preach about? "Tribulation worketh
patience and patience, experience." God allows tribula-
tions so that we can have some experiences! Job attended
ten funerals, lost all of his property, and had a marital
fracas all within a matter of days! Then when he became
physically disabled, his friends came to rebuke him! But
in that low condition, God was with him. His accusers did
not know the nature of grace, forgiveness, identification,
or restoration. We learn about God's nature when we are
down. Micah said that his enemies were in his own
household. Some in the household of faith kick the fallen
instead of helping them back up. While God seeks to heal
the wounded, they break their hearts even more. Two are
better than one only if the one still standing helps the
fallen to his feet.

As long as there is life, there is hope. Sampson fell
into sin and was shorn of his glory by the world. But even
as the three thousand mocked his disfigurement and
defeat, he was calling on the Lord for a return of his
strength and power. Sampson accomplished more in the
hour of his death than all the days of his life. He looked
like he was a victim as he stood chained to the columns,
but he was calling the shots through his prayers as the
object of God's grace. God's plan can work all things
together for good. Circumstances must not be allowed to
control the emotions or dictate how we think in times of
trouble.

God would not let His people mourn more than
thirty days for Moses. His counsel was, "Arise, go over
this Jordan." Moses was dead and they were alive, so they
were to get up and go on. Joshua was intimidated as he
compared himself with his predecessor. But God told him

to take courageous steps of faith with the assurance of certain success.

Sinners become winners in Christ! We are human and so we fail, but that is not the end of the story. Victory is written in the back of the Book. The prodigal blew it but he came back home to be restored. When Cain offered the wrong sacrifice, he was told that the proper sin offering was waiting for him right on his doorstep. Jonah was rebellious but after rejecting his opportunity of obedience, the word of the Lord came to him a second time. In Numbers 21, Israel sinned and was chastened, but even in chastisement, she was given a provision to be spared. The Father's focus is not on what we have done, but on what Christ has done, not on what we are like, but what He is like. Doubting Thomas could not believe that Christ had risen, but Jesus appeared a second time just for him.

All human beings are asked to do is to gaze upon the Son. The precious blood of Jesus Christ has been spilled on our behalf. In heaven, this blood still cries out "Father, forgive them; for they know not what they do!" Interceding on our behalf, Christ vows to perfect all those who belong to Him. As our High Priest, He bears our names on his breast. We have been engraved upon the nail scarred palms of His hands. Our answer to every accusation is the blood of the Lamb. The Completer of the Law has declared us pardoned and beckons us to reign in life through the abundance of grace and the gift of righteousness.

THREE

MORALITY

The Mosaic Law was fulfilled by Jesus Christ, leaving the believer free to live under grace. Now what place does the moral law have? Morality speaks of the rules, principles, and virtues of right and wrong conduct which preserve national entity, social norms, businesses, marriages, and institutions of every sort. Without a moral set of ethics, our world would be in ruin. The honor code requires that we work hard, pay our bills, be faithful in relationships, and respond to all rightful claims on our lives. When morality degenerates, nations disintegrate. Throughout history, civilization's great empires degenerated morally prior to being overthrown nationally.

Today, the breakdown of morality is responsible for many of our current social and medical problems. Religion used to go hand-in-hand with education, developing the moral capacity of the mind along with its perceptual and logical abilities. Children's books always had a moral, a happy or tragic ending, assuring the child of expected consequences according to one's choices and actions. The moral responsibility to help mankind and be of use to society was intentionally inculcated in the hearts of our young.

Morality once governed the subject matter and manner of our newspapers. The freedom of the press to differ, criticize, and inform was governed by journalistic ethics upon which people relied. The public expected that they would not be subjected to reporting which had not been thoroughly researched, including the character and integrity of the sources. A reporter was governed by a genuine desire to know and make known the truth, and the editor adequately directed his employees to that end.

A moral ethic corresponding to every freedom and profession gives the exercise of that freedom and profession its social significance. Moral integrity kept marriages together even when incompatible. A sense of what was right, of what was expected, kept order in the ranks. Morality compelled a man to provide for his wife and family. The wife, in turn, kept the home a place of order and pleasant interaction. This was not always the case, but it was the accepted ideal, the established policy of acting in regard for the welfare of the whole. Morality kept people attending church, working, and paying off obligations without shifting the responsibility to anyone else.

Decency, duty, discipline: these are the words we once associated with morality. Freedoms, being thus attached to morality, did not give the individual the freedom to be immoral. The blue laws were taken seriously and implemented. One could go to jail for a homosexual act or be fined for taking God's name in vain. All this was so because judicial law was derived from moral law which had its source in the Mosaic Law.

Morality, then, has its source in spirituality, the social laws among men being derived from the laws of God. But, does being moral make a person spiritual? Very definitely not. Morality tells me what to do, but spirituality tells me who I am. Today, morality is replacing spirituality in the pulpit. Dead fundamentalism has reduced Christianity to a system of right and wrong, exalting morality and denouncing immorality instead of preaching the royal law of love which fulfills all moral laws and surpasses them. C.S. Lewis humorously pointed out the two dangers of living by a set of rules: if we fail to follow our set routine, we are defeated; if we succeed, we have a deceptively good conscience and feel satisfied with ourselves even in the complete absence of real charity and faith.

Learned Behavior

Seminars, books, cassettes, and booklets today are teaching Christians the A,B,Cs of "Christian" living. As my good friend, Pastor Tom Powell of Tacoma, Washington pointed out to me, this is no more than learned behavior. Christianity must be more than a series of "how-tos!" Bible doctrine is informative, but it cannot be appropriated without the Holy Spirit. Many of the celebrated authors and speakers who promote their packages and programs leave a living God completely out of the picture! Their forty-five points of how to be spiritual, how to have a good marriage, and how to raise the children, are based upon analyzing and changing natural behavior.

People try to take their evil and make it good so they can feel better about themselves. Having a better self-image becomes the business of their lives. But anything that does not proceed out of **God's** goodness falls short of His glory. Knowledge separated from God's life, whether good or evil, is forbidden fruit. We regret our evil doings of the past, forgetting that the good which was devoid of Christ's life was just as evil! True Christian behavior is performed by the life of Christ in us.

As the volition chooses to receive and respond in obedience to His life, **Christ** is magnified, not self-right-eousness. Anything short of this is merely behavior modification. Men learn: "Husbands, do this." Women hear: "Wives, do this." He learns to hold her hand and she tries harder to submit to him, but the marriage is not transformed. Why don't the learned behavioral patterns last? Because neither of them have learned to relate to God! The truth preached in life-giving power gives Christians the ability to love each other without always having to revert back to the letter to enforce correct responses. Morality, family harmony, and effective lifestyles are manifestations of the work of the Spirit.

The information Jesus gave us was meant to be appropriated in the Spirit to become LIFE. Job said, "For he performeth the thing that is appointed for me" (Job 23:14). In the New Testament, Paul said, "Faithful is He that calleth you, who will also do it" (1 Thess. 5:24). Christian behavior is not a formula or a code of ethics, but Christ performing what He asks of us. It is a divine way, not a human standard.

Claiming things in Christ's name can be yet another form of learned behavior. A contrived faith formula rules out sovereignty. Any system in which we can function without the intervening presence of God is simply human performance in Jesus' name. Failing these superfi-cially-imposed behavior programs leaves the Christian with undefined guilt.

Children need enforced discipline and to learn how to behave, but that cannot substitute for a vital relationship with God when they come of age. It is not that there is anything wrong with a program, but there is no life in it, by itself. The knowledge of the truth is not enough. We need divine dynamics!

Pharisaism

Knowledge of what is supposed to be done leaves the soul powerless to do it, and sometimes not even desirous of having it done. Spiritual light is the power behind moral light. When Jesus came to earth, He found that the religious representation had no relationship with heaven. Human standards and traditions had taken the focus off of God and had put it on men. They had ceased to look for a messiah who would come and save them from their sins because their morality deceived them into thinking they did not have any! Sarcastically, Jesus said to them, "I did not come to call the righteous" (Mark 2:17). By living up to their own set of rules and decorum with self-satisfied smugness, they missed the whole point of man's existence. Jesus called them whited tombstones— clean on the outside, but filled with death on the inside.

Morality can be a great counterfeit for spirituality. Being able to keep a standard without God's life produces self-righteousness which compares and condemns others. "I thank thee that I am not as other men are, extortioners, unjust, adulterers, or even as this publican." Thousands of Christians across our nation are congratulating themselves with precisely this sentiment. There is just one problem: the Pharisee who said this in Luke 18:11 was talking to himself. He left his place of worship never having contacted God. The publican, whom he had condemned, wept in acute awareness of his sin and begged God for mercy. It was he who went out justified, having bona fide peace with God.

Who are the upright? The self-righteous ministers who would never dream of falling like their unfortunate "brothers," or those who have fallen and have repented and who are depending upon Christ's life daily not to do it again? "Judge not lest ye be judged!" (Matt. 22:13). It seems that whenever I read or hear about "so-and-so" condemning another preacher or ministry, it is just a matter of time before I hear of the fall of "so-and-so!" The Pharisee lied when he said that he was not as other men. If we say we have no sin, we make God a liar who says that all have sinned. "There hath no temptation taken you but such as is common to man" (1 Cor. 10:13).

The scribes and the Pharisees brought a woman taken in the very act of adultery and set her in the midst of the crowd. Misguided morality always exposes the guilty party in front of everybody. They were just waiting to accuse Christ either of being soft on sin or of being overly authoritative by taking the life of another in His own hands.

Jesus said nothing, but as His finger wrote on the ground, the probing finger of the Holy Spirit was stirring up the mud in their own conscience. None of them were righteous enough to cast the first stone. They left one by one, leaving the guilty party, as it always should be, alone before God.

After Christ forgave her, giving her new power to go and sin no more, His eyes canvassed the crowd. "I am the Light of the world" He said. The Pharisees had been guiding the people by their man-made standards of righteousness as the blind leading the blind. Now Jesus stood before them. "He that followeth Me shall not walk in darkness, but shall have the light of life" (John 8:12). We do not have to settle for morality when we have Jesus! Moral light is not the ultimate light. Moral light can point out failures, but only spiritual light can forgive and restore and empower us not to fail.

What was it about Jesus that angered the Pharisees so? It was the manifestation of His Father's compassion toward the masses and His indictment against relative righteousness. Morality is naturally very comforting because there is always someone who is worse than you are! The disconcerting thing about grace is its claim that we are all in need of it. In John 9, Jesus healed the blind man but He could not heal the Pharisees. "Are we blind, too?" they asked Him. Jesus answered, "If you were blind, you would not be guilty of sin; but now that you claim you can see, your guilt remains." Guilt remains for those who declare they have none.

Jesus told His disciples, "You are light of the world" and then proceeded to dissect the guts of the Law. Murder was reduced to its root cause of anger; sacrifice was declared useless if one was not reconciled to a brother; adultery was identified as being the very first thought or look. No wonder not one of the onlookers could pick up a stone against the one caught in an overt act! Morality in its purest sense is loving exactly the way God loves. "Be ye perfect," Jesus said, "as your heavenly Father is perfect."

The human heart is like the chamber of imagery described in Ezekiel 8:12. Outwardly the temple may seem in order but underground every form of creeping thing, abominable beast, and idol are flashed upon the screen of its walls. Even the ancients worshipped there—the Sanhedrin called to represent the holiness of God. Pharisaism prides itself on tithing down to the minutest grains of mint and cumin but overlooks the weightier matters of the heart. A true understanding of the moral law brings the best man to his knees crying, "Lord, have mercy on me a sinner!" We not only have broken the Mosaic Law against God, but we have fallen short of the moral law of what we owe our brother.

The Christian witness must go beyond the light of conscience which tells us, "someone ought to pay." Someone **has** paid—Jesus Christ. Going beyond a human interpretation of morality, spiritual life picks up the fallen even if it is seven times in a day. This greater light does not produce lawlessness, carelessness, or sin but provides realistic victory over sin because of its own pure life transforming the soul.

Ministers of Righteousness

"Satan himself is transformed into an angel of light. Therefore it is no great thing if his ministers also be transformed as the ministers of righteousness" (2 Cor. 11:14-15). Many men (and today we would have to add, women!) with clerical collars do not have pastors' hearts. They have not come in response to Christ's call to feed His lambs, but they are hirelings, treating their vocation as a business and other churches as the competition. Matthew 23:5-7 perfectly describes these self-made clergy: "But all their works they do for to be seen of men: they make broad their phylacteries, and enlarge the borders of their garments, and love the uppermost rooms at feasts, and the chief seats on the synagogues, and greetings in the markets, and to be called of men, Rabbi, Rabbi." These ministers derive identity from their office, not from God. Religious lust and ego promotion motivates their service.

The Pharisees harassed Jesus because He was a threat to success. When they saw the response of the masses, they said "We'd better do something before we lose our congregations!" (paraphrase of John 12:19). This is the base motive behind the majority of ecclesiastical judging today. It has been said, "Love looks through a telescope; envy, through a microscope!" The smart politician knows how to keep envy out of his voice when he accuses his opponent of fooling the public! Behind much of the indignant cries against the men of God who have failed is the serpent of jealousy. The larger a man's following, the more the competition will demand "justice" if he falls. It is amazing why denominations will get together to agree about who they disagree with! That is what happened with the Sadducees and the Pharisees. They never saw eye to eye except when it came to crucifying their mutual Competitor!

Malcolm X was killed by members of the Nation of Islam, a rival Moslem group. Christian denominations do not stoop so low. They are content to settle for character assassination. The frightening indictment the apostle Paul made concerning ministers of righteousness was that their "ministry" came from the pit of hell! What were their satanic tactics? Their primary goal was to discredit the apostle Paul. They wanted the Corinthian congregation for themselves so they subtly began to win the people over to themselves by vilifying him. That is why Paul had to write to defend his record and character before the whole church. These men made Paul's person the issue. In order to establish themselves as the genuine article, they first had to destroy Paul's standing in Corinth. They had a hidden agenda. Like serpents, they slithered in making personality, not doctrine, the issue. Instead of keeping their eyes fixed upon Christ as Paul had taught them, the Corinthians, like Eve, entertained their sly innuendos.

These false apostles were trafficking religion. They robbed believers of their faith while operating under the guise of credentialed respectability. The religious structure of Paul's time was always the source of his greatest persecution. In Acts 13, they let him speak in their synagogue until they saw how many came out to hear him! Then, they could not rest until they had stirred up the devout women and the chief men of the city to expel him from their coasts. In Acts 14, they spread gossip about him among the Gentiles until a sizable crowd wanted to kill him. Religion, government, and public opinion finally ganged up together to end his life.

The Bible says that we wrestle not against flesh and blood, but against spiritual powers and principalities. This should make us think twice before we listen to indictments made against men of faith. In wartime, one does not turn on a soldier who has gone down but rather rescues him because it was done by enemy fire. In Revelation 12:10, the devil is called "the accuser of the brethren." In James 3:6, the gossiping tongue is said to be "set on fire by hell." If ministers are truly concerned about their congregations, instead of stooping to methods which would spiritually disqualify them from the clergy, they should concentrate on the quality of life offered from their own pulpits. If the congregation is well-fed, they will not look for greener pastures! Preaching the truth will do more than religious crusading.

David sat on the throne of judgment seething with

righteous indignation when he heard of the rich herds-
man who had greedily stolen and killed a poor shepherd's only lamb. But Nathan pointed the finger at him
and said, "Thou art the man!" He was so ready to condemn one whose life perfectly mirrored his own! Judah
angrily called for Tamar, his widowed, pregnant daugh-
ter-in-law, to be brought to him to be burned for her
whoredom. She came bearing the proof of the blame,
saying, "Discern, I pray thee, whose are these, the signet,
the bracelets, and staff." They were Judah's own! By not
wedding her to the next son as he had promised, he had
driven her to disguise herself and play the harlot. He,
himself, had fathered the child! His secret sin was exposed when he set himself up as judge.

> You can advertise your virtues,
> You can self-achievement laud,
> You can load yourself with riches,
> But you can't fool God!
> —G. Kleiser

FOUR

HUMAN WEAKNESS

God had a purpose for creating man lower than the angels and then allowing him to fall. He permitted Satan to infiltrate the Garden of Eden and to bring man under the power of death. God's purpose was to glorify himself by means of man's frailty! His character of grace is best revealed to men and to angels through the medium of weakness.

Before humans were ever created, Lucifer found fault with God. In response to Satan's charges, God chose what He knew would become a fallen race to manifest His nature of love in the deepest way. The serpent's first charge against God to Eve was that He was withholding something good from her. Satan always tries to deny the goodness of God. But God's plan is to reveal the goodness of His character. Human failure is not an obstacle to the revelation of the manifold grace of God, but its very means! Grace finds its ultimate expression by going out to the worst. In Heaven, the presence of the bride of Christ, the Church, will magnify God's grace for all eternity because none of us will deserve to be there! Yes, God commended His own love when He died for sinners.

Once under the government of grace, we glorify God by continually receiving what we do not deserve. Grace gives us a life outside of our own to experience power beyond our natural limitations and express fruits beyond our natural production. Our eternal purpose in the devil's world is to reveal the character of God's goodness in the midst of our own inadequacy. The apostle Paul prayed that our eyes would be opened to this mighty purpose and to the power which comes from Christ.

We are testimonies of God's endless love. Our position in grace will testify of God's perfect justice at the last judgment, making it obvious that the demons and the lost had to reject grace in order to go to hell. Sin will not send them there, but their own rejection of the unlimited Atonement and the Person of love. They could have received the free gift extended to all. There will be weeping and gnashing of teeth, for everyone in hell will have rejected the free gift.

The Power of Grace

Grace is our teacher (Titus 2:12). We do not need a multitude of laws and rules if we are taking advantage of the access to God which grace has given us. Grace teaches us to deny initiations from Satan's kingdom. Like a mother nourishing her child, the Spirit nourishes us with the milk of God's Word as we rest in the arms of the Son. His gentleness makes us great as He teaches us to appropriate the power which He has made available to us. He understands our genetics, our upbringing, the forces in our environment, and the opposition against us as He patiently teaches us how to have the victory in Him.

The church of Ephesus in Revelation 2:1-5 was upright morally but not pure spiritually because of having left her grace premise. "Herein is love, not that we loved God, but that He loved us" (1 John 4:10). Though Ephesus did many wonderful works, she had left her first love— her consciousness of God's love for her as her motive for living. Our works do not glorify God if they are not done in response to and complete dependence upon His life in us. The Spirit of God calls, "Come away, My love"—out from denominational camps, possessive relationships, personality syndromes, and external demands—into a living relationship of dependence upon Him, alone.

When Adam and Eve fell, they became separated from the experience of who God was. They entered into a works program, sewing fig leaves to cover up their inadequacy. Redemption has brought us back into right relationship with God so that we can worship Him for who He really is and let Him be our life. Mental health is the state of operating in the consciousness of the love of God. "For God hath not given us the spirit of fear; but of power, and of love, and of a sound mind" (2 Tim. 1:7). When we are securely established in the love of God as the foundation of our identity and relationship with Him, we do not need the security system of a set of rules to maintain our acceptance.

God does not give us strength to remain the same, but He progressively weakens us so that we will accept our co-crucifixion and resurrection in Christ. Severe trials are appointed to individuals, families, churches, and nations as God tests the quality of the internal foundation. Every disciple in the garden of Gethsemane forsook Jesus in their hour of testing. He had chosen them because they were weak. They had to be confronted with that weakness and be brought to the end of themselves before they could be used.

In Genesis 32, Jacob wrestled the angel through the night. God waited until he had spent all of his natural strength and could only cleave to the angel. Leaning on Him in utter exhaustion, Jacob received the blessing. The apostle Paul wrestled with a personal problem which left him in a weakened state. When he besought the Lord to remove it, God's answer was: "My grace is sufficient for thee: for My strength is made perfect in weakness" (2 Cor. 12:9). Paul learned to glory in his infirmities which made him depend on God's power. His release came when he realized "when I am weak, then am I strong." We build walls to retain what little strength we have instead of relying on the pure grace of God. Jacob, weaned of his manipulating ways, was the strongest when the weakest. At the last—weak, blind, and dying—he had a supernatural blessing to give.

We need to stop resisting the weakening process! Natural strength must be uprooted before we can be established in grace. Will we prop up old Adam, or will we let him die and enjoy resurrection? Being uprooted is a painful process because the old "I" hangs on to the only identity it has ever known.

The Identity Crisis

Crisis is when the bottom of our self-support systems is kicked out from under us. Crisis is the unveiling of our weakness, and can often come in the form of failure. Failure can be the most important event and blessing in disguise for the believer. The greatest ingredient for growth is need! The Lord has a program which allows us to fail. The more self-righteous we are, the greater that fall will be! Failure produces need which leads to hunger which drives us to Christ. Miles J. Stanford writes, "Our personal, heart-breaking failure in every phase of our Christian life is our Father's preparation for His success on our behalf." What Stanford calls "negative processing" brings us into utter reliance on the positive promises of God. As he observes, "We all began in sheer grace and we must continue and arrive on the same basis."[1] The lessons we learned at our spiritual birth have to be learned repeatedly in spiritual growth and service.

The true value of something is not known until it is needed and wanted. Peter needed to fail so that he could understand those who fail. He needed failure to make him hungry for the power of God. He needed failure to lose confidence in himself. He needed failure to become hungry not to fail. "Lovest thou Me?" Jesus asked. Failure reduced him to this basic question. He had to be reduced so that God could lead him in his future ministry without the interference of self-interest or an inflated sense of self-importance. He had to learn how to be carried by the Lord. Out of the crisis of failure came capacity, maturity, experience, comfort, wisdom, knowledge, and oneness with Christ.

Simon the Pharisee judged the repentant harlot who washed Christ's feet with her tears. But the one who had been forgiven the most loved the most. Her failure led to hunger. Her hunger led her to Christ. Great was her failure and great was her faith. Being stripped and left in personal bankruptcy leads to healing and restoration as we experience the depravity of self and the true value of humility, grace, and Christ's life within.

Abraham's failure with Hagar was part of the growing process which led him to his faith on Mt. Moriah with

Isaac. Paul, the "chief of sinners," became the chief apostle who wrote the bulk of the New Testament. Humbled by his violent acts against Christ and the Church, he became an effective servant who fed the flock. Every leader must know what it is to be a lamb carried by the Chief Shepherd. The inner experience of grace produces an interaction of love. The desire to be like Christ grows out of the crisis which causes disillusionment with self.

If crisis does not smash the self-righteous complex that has developed over the years to defend and preserve self, the Christian carries a spiritual disease without even knowing it. Absalom is a perfect example of this. For years he harbored a grudge against his father, David, for not dealing with his brother Amnon's crime of rape against his sister. Taking justice into his own hands and killing Amnon did not satisfy Absalom's reactionary drive. The virus of self-deception is progressively destructive. His contagion spread until it became conspiratorial. He enticed the people to follow him and then finally went to war against his father. His self-righteous complex destroyed his own potential. He refused to be weakened and humbled, thus in the end he was killed as a victim of the battle his own reaction set into motion.

Emotional Reaction in Crisis

Crisis brings out a panoply of paranoias in the natural, adamic man. We may think people dislike us or are talking about us because past, unresolved guilt is being projected toward the people in our present circumstances. Grandiose paranoia causes some to think they are geniuses or prophets or have some other highly-elevated calling. Jealous paranoia drives some to be over-protective of what and who "belongs" to them. Erotic paranoia sends others into the euphoric "sense" of who they are going to marry or into an overpowering attraction to another individual. Desire and need form a powerful, subjective voice that seems to be God. Others experience projected paranoia, becoming angry to escape an overwhelming sense of self-condemnation. Strong, unconscious feelings of inadequacy hidden in the subjective mind surface in crisis, perverting themselves in an amazing array of self-defense mechanisms. Projections and distortions protect the soul from confronting the inner conflict which promises so much pain. Repression erupts in reaction as the pan finally boils over.

When this happens, the sympathy and protection of others is needed. While in this state of hypersensitivity and emotional spasm, a person requires an atmosphere of love and understanding in order to be free to express the dominating hurts, needs, and questions. Communication without fear or insecurity is vital for honest growth. In an environment of unconditional acceptance, the conscious mind can sort through the projections erupting from the involuntary mind. God says, "Counsel is Mine, and sound wisdom: I am understanding: I have strength" (Prov. 8:14).

Though the soul seeks to escape this unmasking of its inherent weakness, facing our nothingness is the best thing that can ever happen to us. In the light, God replaces the hurt and emptiness with His Word and Spirit. The Comforter covers us in the heights of our depths. Failure is only lasting when we do not turn to God in our low points. Elijah became self-destructive in the depths of his depression but he ran to the mount and found peace through the still, small voice of God as he poured his heart out to Him. The promises became real as he found the

God of the valleys.

If the prominent Christian figures who failed in recent years had known the God of the valley and the unconditional love of the body of Christ, they would have found help for their problems before those problems destroyed them. All too often, indictment and rejection await the failing Christian so that he never dares to be honest with himself or others. Leaders are left with no place to go. They have a right to be healed and restored just like everybody else. It is a family matter that should be handled within the church and never exposed to the secular world.

FIVE

THE SPIRITUAL WAR

Maybe you will remember this story: In the late 1970s a Japanese soldier was found in the jungle of a Pacific island. For almost thirty years this man thought World War II was still being fought. Consequently, those who found him had a difficult time persuading him to "surrender!" He did not know the war was over. Many people do not know that the spiritual war is over. Some never even knew there was one was going on!

The arena in which this war began, perhaps millions of years ago, was in the spiritual world. It had its roots in an internal rebellion. Lucifer, "son of the morning," the anointed cherub of God, turned against God. "For thou hast said in thine heart, I will ascend into heaven, I will exalt my throne above the stars of God: I will also sit upon the mount of the congregation, in the sides of the north: I will ascend above the heights of the clouds; I will be like the most High" (Isa. 14:12-14). Lucifer was not content with his high rank among the angels. He wanted to be over all, including God. The ensuing power struggle between the two kingdoms which involved the angels who sided with Lucifer and those who remained true to God was very much to affect planet Earth.

It was after the war in the heavenlies had begun that God created Adam's race. The serpent in the Garden of Eden was used to beguile Eve with the poison of pride. She was promised to be like God if she disobeyed God. This was a crucial stage in the war. If by her free will she rejected the serpent's initiations, Lucifer ("that old serpent called the devil, and Satan, which deceiveth the whole world" Rev. 12:9) would have no means of access to the human race. But if she submitted to the temptation with Adam's acquiescence, the devil would become their head and they would unwittingly be joined to his forces.

A negative choice was made and Satan, fallen Lucifer, assumed headship of fallen humanity. Adam and Eve repented of their choice and were forgiven as individuals, but they could not buy back the territory they had given to the enemy. They could not retrieve the title deed which they had sold by their disobedience. This accounts for the titles of rulership which the Bible attributes to Satan: "god of this world" (2 Cor. 4:4), "prince of the power of the air" (Eph. 2:2), and "spiritual wickedness in high places" (Eph. 6:12). Being under the devil in rank and power, man could not rectify the situation.

But right in the midst of the original defeat, God foretold the means of Satan's future demise: "I will put enmity between thee and the woman, and between thy seed and her seed; it shall bruise thy head, and thou shall bruise his heel!" The snake's low position and man's dominion over him was to be a picture of an ultimate doom: God would send the Messiah, born of a woman, to crush the spiritual serpent's head. Satan bruised Christ's heel at the Cross, but the devil's right of headship over man was smashed forever. This was Christ's purpose in coming to die. When He spoke of the Cross in Matthew 16, his "friend" Peter tried to talk Him out of it. Instead of being comforted by Peter's words, Jesus replied: "Get thee behind Me, **Satan!**" Just earlier, Peter had been used as God's mouthpiece proclaiming Christ's heavenly Sonship. Now, moments later, he was used as an instrument of Satan in an attempt to dissuade Jesus from His purpose.

War is a bloody, ugly enterprise. Many times the demonic forces tried to kill Jesus through the Pharisees. Jesus told them: "Ye are of your father the devil, and the lusts of your father ye will do. He was a murderer from the beginning" (John 8:44). But they accused Jesus of being of the devil and took up stones to kill Him. Again, in John 10, they took up stones to kill Him but, again, He escaped out of their hands. The last months of His ministry, the disciples lived in constant fear for His life. The eve before the day of the final battle, Jesus was in the Garden of Gethsemane. His right-hand men were sleeping at their posts under a supernatural oppression as the Son of Man faced Satan's last attempts to murder Him before reaching the Cross. He cried out to the Father three times, "let this cup pass from Me!" Was it fear of death? I think not. In John 12, He had already faced that issue and said, "What shall I say? Father save me from this hour: But for this cause came I unto this hour." Jesus was grappling in spiritual hand-to-hand combat an onslaught of the demonic host trying to take His life. An angel was sent from heaven to strengthen Him. Blood dropped from His pores, so close did the struggle come to death. At the last, He prevailed. He then woke His disciples and went to meet Judas Iscariot who was leading the temple guards to Him. Jesus told them, "this is your hour and the power of darkness."

The Pharisees ultimately achieved their murderous ends, not realizing that in doing so, they were fulfilling the perfect will of God. Peter would declare in the first sermon of Pentecost, "Him, being delivered by the determinate counsel and foreknowledge of God, ye have taken, and by wicked hands have crucified and slain" (Acts 2:23). It was all according to the battle plan. Hanging on the Cross, having given His last orders which included a pardon to the thief beside Him, Jesus was forsaken by the Father as He identified with all of man's sins going back to the first cause of Adam. As He cried out: "It is finished!", His heel was bruised and Satan's headship was crushed.

Christ's Victory

> Christ when He died
> Deceived the cross,
> And on Death's side
> Threw all the loss:
> The captive world awak'd and found
> The prisoners loose, the jailer bound.
> O dear and sweet dispute
> 'Twixt Death's and Love's far different
>   fruit,
> Different as far
> As antidote and poisons are:
> By the first fatal Tree
> Both life and liberty
> Were sold and slain,
> By this they both look up, and live again.

O strange and mysterious strife
Of open death and hidden life:
When on the cross my King did bleed,
Life seemed to die, Death died indeed.
                    —Richard Crashaw[1]

On the third day, Christ rose from the grave, having proclaimed His triumph to the underworld, and took His blood to heaven as proof of the victorious fulfillment of God's requirements for redemption. The Levitical offerings foreshadowed this great event. "But when Christ appeared as a high priest of the good things to come, He entered through the greater and more perfect tabernacle, not made with hands, that is to say, not of this creation; and not through the blood of goats and calves, but through His own blood. He entered the holy place once for all, having obtained eternal redemption" (Heb. 9:11-12; NASB). By clearing man's name of the original sin, Christ reclaimed Satan's stronghold on earth.

Ephesians 4:8 describes the success and supremacy of Christ's ascension: "When He ascended up on high, He led captivity captive." Colossians 2:15 says, "having spoiled principalities and powers, He made a shew of them openly, triumphing over them in it." Because the nature of man's fall was spiritual, first, but included the biological repercussions of physical sickness and death, before we could experience any of the earthly benefits of restoration to God, Christ had to accomplish these things in the heavenlies. That is why the Bible says that we are blessed with all spiritual blessings in heavenly places; that we have been delivered from the invisible power of darkness and spiritually translated into the kingdom of God's dear Son. Tactically, positional victory had to be won in heaven before experiential reconciliation on earth could be received. That is why our salvation is **not** conditioned by our state. It is "an inheritance incorruptible, and undefiled and that fadeth not away, reserved in heaven" (1 Pet. 1:4). Being temporarily backslidden in time cannot touch what has been purchased and imputed to our account forever in heaven. It was a transaction made by God, Himself, in agreement with His own terms.

The Apostle Paul's mission was to make all men see this victory "which He wrought in Christ, when He raised Him from the dead, and set Him at His own right hand in the heavenly places, far above all principality and power, and might, and dominion, and every name that is named, not only in this world, but also in that which is to come: and hath put all things under His feet, and gave Him to be the head over all things to the church, which is His body, the fullness of Him that filleth all in all" (Eph. 1:20-23, 3:8-9). In ascending, Christ gave His Church—all who would believe that He was the Christ, the Son of the Living God—an exalted position over the devil. In that position, she has delegated authority to bind and release on earth all issues which have heavenly sources."

How the Church uses or abuses her authority determines much of what happens in world affairs. The Church has a definite identity before the invisible forces and a sacred mission to fulfill. Many "captives" are hiding out, just like the Japanese man, who do not know that the war is over and who the Victor is. If the devil can keep these poor ignorants in the dark, or better yet, cause the victorious opposition to oppose each other, his defeat will not seem so final. Our vanquished foe continues to stalk the planet like a lion "seeking whom he may devour" until that conclusive hour when Christ returns to claim the territory rightfully His. Until we see the fulfillment of

Ephesians 1:14, the crowning "redemption of the purchased possession," our responsibility is to maintain the
freedom Christ died to provide and herald its proclama-
tion to all who have not heard.

Project: Alienation

Having lost the battle to alienate God from men,
Satan wants to alienate men from God and from each
other. If he can convince the captives that they are too
sinful to be saved, and that the messenger is too sinful to
be trusted, no one will respond to the news of the great
emancipation. Failure is magnified by the powers of
darkness, whether they be our own failures or the fall of
others, so that Christ's victory will be overshadowed. In
light of this ultimate satanic purpose, doctrinal Christians are wary about receiving accusations against other
Christians. Jesus gives them good news to spread. Anyone spreading bad news is not of the same Spirit.

Unfortunately, this is what happens: the world
spreads a story about a Bible-believing church. Another
Bible-believing church hears the story and believes it. In
order to protect the congregation from the supposed bad
influence of the first church, the second church tells all of
its membership. The second church may have "good"
motives, but is sadly ignorant of satanic warfare. *Diabolos*
means slanderer. This is the "liar from the beginning"
that Jesus was so angry about. Pious Pharisees served the
devil's cause by spreading his accusations, criticisms,
and innuendos. That is why the apostles continually
warned their flocks against gossip. "Speak not evil one of
another, brethren" (James 4:11); "Against an elder, receive not an accusation, but before two or three witnesses" (1 Tim. 5:19); "Let no corrupt communication

proceed out of your mouth, but that which is good to the use of edifying, that it may minister grace unto the hearers" (Eph. 4:29); "He that saith he is in the light, and hateth his brother, is in darkness" (1 John 2:9). A frustrated, defeated serpent wants to hurt God by hurting those who belong to Him. Discord hurts the One he can never be like. It only takes a little leaven of malice for Satan to infiltrate God's work.

Joseph said to his brothers after they had miserably failed him, "Fear not: for am I in the place of God?" Satan, the usurper, would like us to assume a role of judgment not rightfully ours, which belongs only to God. We have every right to diligently search the doctrine and the fruit of a church we might be considering joining. But anything further than that enters into the system of evil. The Christian's mind is to be occupied with things which are true, honest, just, pure, lovely, and of good report. "If there be any virtue, and if there be any praise, think on **these** things" (Phil. 4:8). It is better to think too positively than to risk being infected mentally and emotionally by negativity which has its source in another kingdom. The Lord Jesus' Spirit is a Lamb's Spirit. He is our supreme example of meekness. As we apron ourselves with His humility, we protect ourselves from the master of pride.

> Walk worthy of the vocation wherewith ye are called, with all lowliness and meekness, with longsuffering, forbearing one another in love (Eph. 4:1-2).

Religion

Those who profess the name of Christ are capable of counteracting His purposes. Jesus said to self-professed

Bible scholars, "Go ye and learn what that meaneth, I will have mercy, and not sacrifice" (Matt. 9:13). The Pharisees had taken it upon themselves, as the "experts," to pronounce judgment in the place of the most High. Jesus says to the religious world, "go and learn"! Go back to the Book which you profess to represent and read Hosea 6:6, Isaiah 49:13, and Micah 6:8, you interpreters of the Law! Go back to the prophets which you claim to embrace. Search the Scriptures to find the One whom you have overlooked! Ceremony means nothing without mercy. Christ did not come to call the righteous, but sinners to repentance!

This Christ has called His ministers to administer forgiveness. "Be ye kind to one another, tenderhearted, forgiving one another, even as God for Christ's sake hath forgiven you" (Eph. 4:32). By this foot-washing love, Jesus said we would be known as His disciples. We are called, not only to give intellectual and verbal assent to the death, burial and resurrection, but to deeply identify with the inward ills and outward effects of the troubles and sufferings, the sins and the failures of mankind.

The Pharisees were shocked to find the Son of God eating with the disreputables, but Jesus asked, "Where else should I be?" It is the sick who are in need of the physician. When Christ saw the needs of the multitude, He was moved with compassion. Feeding the hungry, healing the sick, forgiving the fallen, encouraging the poor—this was His Father's business. "Have mercy on me, O Lord, thou Son of David" (Matt. 15:22). Even the Gentiles found mercy at the hands of this Jewish Messiah. The Syrophenecian woman sought the crumbs which had fallen from the children's table. Not only did the big needs move Jesus, but every need; not just the crisis, but also the details of life.

Dead religion is abstract and hostile. Insidious in its harmfulness, it burdens man, misrepresenting God to those searching for the truth. Christ saw men and women as helpless sheep without a shepherd, driven by those who did not care for their souls. He was angry that they had been mistreated and misinformed. See Jesus addressing the woman who had been excommunicated from the temple and ostracized from society: He calls her "daughter" (Matt. 9:22; NASB). The name penetrates the hearing heart. She was accepted in the Beloved, made a member of the heavenly family by faith.

> To the one refuge she had flown,
> The Godhead's burning flame!
> Of all earth's women she alone
> Hears there the tenderest name.
>
> "Daughter" He said, "be of good cheer;
> Thy faith hath made thee whole":
> With plenteous love, not healing mere
> He comforteth her soul.
> —George McDonald[2]

Christ calls us by name. He numbers every hair, bottles every tear, records every step because we are the objects of His love. Christ gazed over Jerusalem and wept. He saw those created in God's image in a fallen state of depravity.

> Like as a father pitieth his children, so the Lord pitieth them that fear Him. For He knoweth our frame; He remembereth that we are dust (Psalm 103:13-14).

Christ needs His church to be filled with His Spirit in the midst of men's needs. From place to place, person to person, Christ was moved with compassion. His meat was to see men and women come to the saving knowledge of Who He really was. His kind of love heals the inside and corrects the outside. Those who bear His name are to be sons of mercy, moved by the same Spirit which moved Him.

We are not in God's place of judgment, but in Christ's stead as ambassadors of reconciliation. As stewards of grace in the midst of a satanic siege, we have to remember to stay on the winning side. The One we serve died to forgive sinners and ever lives to intercede for them. Everyone has some degree of need for that intervening love. We have been called to give it.

> He held the pitcher—stooping low
> To lips of little ones below,
> Then raised it to the weary saint
> And bade him drink when sick and faint!
> They drank—the pitcher thus between,
> The hand that held it scarce was seen.
>   —Anonymous

SIX

GENUINE TRANSFORMATION

But grow in grace, and in the knowledge of our
Lord and Saviour Jesus Christ. 2 Peter 3:18

A little girl prepared a spaghetti and meatball dinner
for her father. At the table, he looked in shock at the plate
on which his dinner was served. "My dear, this is the cat's
dish," he told his daughter. "But I washed it," was her
reply. "Doesn't matter, dear; this is his plate and it
belongs to him alone!" This funny incident related by a
friend illustrates the biblical principle of sanctification. In
the father's mind, the plate belonged to the cat. Washing
the plate did not change it. There would have to be a
demonstratively significant change in the plate for it to be
acceptable to Dad!

Similarly, man is entirely unacceptable to God outside of being cleansed through an exchanged life at Cal-

vary. Biblical sanctification occurs in three stages: positional, progressive, and ultimate. At salvation, the believer receives the immediate action of being set apart unto God. This is the positional, one-time everlasting separation of the Christian from his identity as a citizen of the kingdom of darkness to his citizenship in the kingdom of Jesus Christ. The Bible often refers to Christians as "saints," which means "set apart ones." Evans, in his book *Great Doctrines of the Bible*, states, "If a man is not a saint, he is not a Christian; if he is a Christian, he is a saint. In some quarters people are canonized after they are dead; the New Testament canonizes believers while they are alive!"

The final form of sanctification will find the believer complete in every way when, at the rapture of the Church, "we shall be like Him." The trump shall sound and He will "change our vile body, that it may be fashioned like unto His glorious body, according to the working whereby He is able even to subdue all things unto Himself" (Phil. 3:21). In the meantime, until that final day, the Christian living on the earth is being progressively sanctified in a process of spiritual growth.

Salvation does not eradicate the old sin nature which wars with the new life of the Spirit in the believer. The ongoing aspect of spiritual growth involves learning how to manifest our heavenly position in our experience as we yield daily to the Lordship of Christ, the power of the Holy Spirit, and the Word of God. Jesus illustrated the difference between positional and progressive sanctification in John 13 when He knelt to wash the disciples' feet. "Thou shalt never wash my feet," Peter protested. Jesus answered, "If I wash thee not, thou hast no part with Me." Peter changed his mind "Lord, not my feet only, but also my hands and my head"! But Jesus said, "He that is washed needeth not save to wash his feet, but is clean every whit." In other words, Peter had already been positionally sanctified, set apart for God. But his feet would need to be washed again and again. Feet speak of our day-to-day walk with the Lord. Just as Peter, walking through the dust and dung of Judaea in that day needed to wash his feet often, spiritually we walk through the muck and mire of a corrupt world. We fail, we sin, we make wrong decisions because we are human. But we do not have to remain in the dust. We can come to Jesus in prayer and find Him in His Word and have our feet cleansed. Through an ongoing walk with Him, we become conformed to His image and develop that maturity of character which glorifies Him.

"If we confess our sins, He is faithful and just to forgive us our sins, and to cleanse us from all unrighteousness" (1 John 1:9). God made a provision for our times of stumbling. In His omniscience, He foreknew the times we would fail. There are growing pains in the maturation process as we learn to decrease and let Christ increase in our lives. But when we fall, we do not have to stay down. The only real failures are those who fall and refuse to stand up again. "For a just man falleth seven times, and riseth up again" (Prov. 24:16).

I know an alcoholic who came to Christ, yet found his habit hard to break. Though he failed even after his conversion, he never lost hope. He kept believing that God was bigger than his sin. Each time of failure was followed by repentance and encouragement from the church as we continued to love and pray for him. Finally, a few years later, he took his last drink. He testifies that he has not taken a drink, now, for over fifteen years.

On the other hand, a famous radio evangelist in the Northeast failed and became so discouraged that he refused to get back up. Because he felt unloved and rejected, he continued to drink, then he turned to drugs, and eventually took his own life. It was a sad ending for a gifted Christian. I often wonder whether a loving response from a few brothers in the faith would have stopped this man's path of self-destruction. Too often, Christians do not want to be contaminated by fellowshipping with someone who has fallen, even if repentance is there. There is One who stands for us no matter what we do. Jesus Christ is our advocate before God, the Father. He represents us even when we are guilty. Our position in Christ is never in jeopardy, being eternal through His finished work.

> My little children, these things write I unto you, that ye sin not. And if any man sin, we have an advocate with the Father, Jesus Christ the righteous: and He is the propitiation for our sins: and not for our's only, but also for the sins of the whole world (1 John 2:1-2).

Grace is our means of growth. Even if we sin outright, we can always turn back to God. "Let the wicked forsake his way, and the unrighteous man his thoughts: and let him return unto the Lord, and He will have mercy upon him; and to our God, for He will abundantly pardon" (Isa. 55:7).

In the fifteenth chapter of John's gospel, known to many as the "vine" chapter, Jesus uses the metaphor of a grapevine to explain spiritual principles of growth. "Abide in Me, and I in you. As the branch cannot bear fruit of itself, unless it abides in the vine, so neither can you, unless you abide in Me. I am the vine, you are the branches; he who abides in Me, and I in him, he bears much fruit; for apart from Me you can do nothing. If anyone does not abide in Me, he is thrown away as a branch, and dries up; and they gather them, and cast them into the fire, and they are burned. If you abide in Me, and My words abide in you, ask whatever you wish, and it shall be done for you" (John 15:4-7; NASB). The word "abide" means to stay in place, to remain in a specific sphere. Our positional standing is "in Christ." Ideally, Jesus would have us remain constantly in His sphere of influence in our earthly experience.

How do we do this? John, in his opening chapter, spoke of Christ as the "Word made flesh." God's Word is more than just His communication to us; it is His very life. To abide in Christ means to stay in His Word and remain in the sphere of its influence. This truth connotes the importance of the local church. Every Christian should be an active member of a church where the Word of God is preached in its entirety. Our relationship with the Bible is vital to growth. Not surprisingly, the Bible's longest chapter is Psalm 119, containing 176 verses exalting God's Word and its benefits. The Word of God guides, protects, purifies, empowers, encourages, and delivers! Those who abide in the Word and submit to the transformation process become great men and women in the kingdom of God, producing much spiritual fruit.

The Apostle Peter had to go through various stages of growth which were often embarrassingly right before the public eye. Bona fide change involves the conversion of the mind, not just outwardly conforming to a new set of standards. Progressive sanctification means being a partaker of God's own nature through accelerated faith in

His promises.

The combination of grace plus knowledge makes the Word of God digestible to the human soul. Knowledge of the letter, alone, can kill human capacity. If the mentality reverts back to a schoolmaster relationship with the Law, there will be no maturing into spiritual sonship. Knowledge alone is not sufficient. We know no truth as we ought to know it until what we know possesses our being. Thousands taught by the Scriptures never let them take over the soul. When God's Word inhabits the human heart, it produces a spiritual celebration within. "Let the word of Christ dwell in you richly in all wisdom; teaching and admonishing one another in psalms and hymns and spiritual songs, singing with grace in your hearts to the Lord" (Col. 3:16).

We can become so locked into the externals that we neglect allowing a living God to speak to the spirit and write upon the heart. Preoccupation with the rate of our own growth can take the joy out of our salvation experience. Theology is not enough. Paul, himself, said "with my mind I myself serve the law of God; but with the flesh the law of sin" (Rom. 7:25). His doctrine was flawless but he had yet to learn how to trust the One he longed to serve. There is a rest for the people of God, a cessation from one's own labors. When Paul discovered the secret of faith-rest, he was able to physically work many more hours of the day because his energy was not consumed by tension and nervous activity. The issue is the operation of God's own life, not the regulation of the outward manifestation. Without receiving God's life, our programs are only attempts to manipulate dead flesh!

"Come unto Me, all ye that labor and are heavy laden and I will give you rest" (Matt. 11:28). Christ came to call us away from a life of unfruitful, religious drudgery. We have to accept the fact that we are humans in a gradual process, instead of trying to please a manufactured image of God which we can never satisfy. The propensity of the flesh is to try to self-atone. The work has been finished. The process is learning to let the splendor of a risen Lord shine from within the vessel. An incorruptible seed is germinating in the midst of the corruptible. The cross we take up daily is our identification with what has been done and Who lives within. It is an adventure of learning mercy from faith to faith and glory to glory. From promise to promise and from glimpse to glimpse, the Spirit of the Lord is changing us into His image.

The Law condemns, exacting a payment we can never give. But we are dead to that standard which has caused so much subjective guilt! We work out our salvation with the new revelation of God's grace. "There is therefore now no condemnation" (Rom. 8:1). We can dance on the dust of the coffin in total liberation because we are married to Another! "Let us labor therefore to enter into that rest" (Heb. 4:11). It is still a labor, because we have to wrestle with our own unbelief. Our humanity does not readily accept all that Christ has for us, thereby limiting its experience to a process. But even when we fail to believe as we know we should, God loves us anyway! If our hearts condemn us, He is greater than the human heart!

A Transformed Ego

In Mark 6:31, Jesus said, "Come ye yourselves apart... and rest a while." If we do not come apart, we will come apart! Grace beckons, but will we come? In order to run the spiritual race, excess baggage must be left behind. Over the years, a self-made ego structure has been built. This ego defends and drives us, substituting for the voice of God. Those who do not have a strong ego keep life at arm's length. To them, everything is abstract, impersonal, and lonely. Negative ego is when the sense of self has been developed in reaction to authority. People pleasers do the opposite, living in the image others project toward them. They are displaced non-persons though they may seem very well adjusted and hardworking. Workaholics sometimes fall into this category. Most marriages fail because the two individuals involved do not know who they really are. The ego, or non-ego, developed from childhood is a weight that keeps Christians from spontaneously responding to grace in an uninhibited growth process. Pressure from the pulpit and well-meaning brothers and sisters in Christ can keep others on the treadmill of anxiety so they never truly enter the race. An overemphasis on rules challenges the adamic nature, bringing back reflections and old responsive patterns of the subjective mind.

People required to conform and perform may eventually react. A non-person cannot perform the duties of a true person. Growth means becoming the unique individuals that God has made us to be. The conception of who we think we are and how we have always been must be laid aside so that we can experience personal growth in response to knowledge of a gracious Person. There is sacrifice in change. The old must give way to the new. Jesus told us to eat His flesh and drink His blood (John 6:53). As an individual, I must saturate my psyche with the consciousness of Jesus Christ—Who He is and what He had done for **me**. The love of God must become personal. Consecration to a brand new perception of identity through the Word of God will develop a new self-image in the dark room of the imagination. This new ego, based on unchanging truth, is able to live before God and love others, having found true security and significance.

Failure can be the catalyst to a once-and-for-all changeover. A pastor's wife was caught stealing. The ministry in her husband's new church had been thriving, the only problem being a lack of funds. Because she identified so strongly with his need, her ego being wrapped up in the church's potential success or failure, she rationalized a plan to "borrow" a large amount of cash to which she had access. When the theft was discovered, it was treated as a major scandal. She, herself, was shocked into the realization of the depth of her own depravity. The hour of crisis forced her to admit she had no righteousness. But, in all reality, she never did!

Guilt, heartache, and inner struggle come from trying to establish some measure of human righteousness. "For they being ignorant of God's righteousness, and going about to establish their own righteousness, have not submitted themselves unto the righteousness of God" (Rom. 10:3). This zeal without knowledge attributed to an unbelieving Israel exists in the Church of Jesus Christ. God allows unusual and embarrassing things to happen so that we will realize that we are nothing without Him. While men strut their qualifications based upon the measurements of comparison, God is not impressed by relative righteousness. The only ones He can bless are those who acknowledge themselves to be bankrupt— those who are ready to be blessed by unmerited favor, alone.

Man puts that which is broken aside, but God puts

that which is unbroken aside. Pride is a stumblingblock which inhibits a true work of God. "Take up the stumbling block out of the way of My people. For thus saith the high and lofty One that inhabiteth eternity, whose name is Holy; I dwell in the high and holy place, with him also that is of a contrite and humble spirit, to revive the spirit of the humble, and to revive the heart of the contrite ones" (Isa. 57:14-15).

The pastor's wife had to realize that even before she took the money, she had no righteousness. "What hast thou that thou didst not receive?" (1 Cor. 4:7). Any position, talent, or fellowship which the Christian enjoys are gifts given by grace, as is the righteousness we possess in Christ. Progressive spirituality comes through progressive humility of response to the promises of grace. As we commune with Christ's mind, more and more of the 7,837 promises contained in the Bible become our personal property through faith appropriation in the frame of reference. "He sent His Word and healed them" (Ps. 107:20). The objective nature of God filling our subjective consciousness empowers our humanity with the Presence of divinity.

A woman listening to my radio broadcast was under unusual stress. Her husband had left her and the whole family was falling apart. Because of her desperate straits, when she heard the message of God's unconditional love and faithfulness, she breathed it in like it was food from heaven. All she had were promises but they built her up in faith. While she was experiencing this process of spiritual restoration, her husband was seriously hurt in a car accident. He came home after being in the hospital many weeks and they were reconciled. She had need of patience but she believed the God of all grace in back of each promise.

God meets the one who is so far down that he will listen to a promise. Only when we have lost all hope in flesh and blood are we willing to adventure onto a brand new pathway of thinking. Some Christians are afraid if their old frame of reference dies, there will be no resurrection! Religious ego is exhausting. The ego is put to better use in personally receiving God's promises than in trying to control behavior and situations.

Sometimes our experience seems dark. Job did not understand the process he was in but he said, "He knoweth the way that I take." We will not always be on a glorious mountaintop but we can learn to trust God in the valley. Job had esteemed God's Word more than his necessary food. He knew that he was in the center of God's will and that, somewhere, God was in his darkness.

From the mount of transfiguration to the pandemonium below where they were unable to cast out a troublesome demon, the disciples experienced both the glory of Christ's deity in their midst and the depravity of their human condition. They had experiences of faith and of faithlessness. The transformed ego is not intimidated by its own inadequacy, but just keeps looking to the light, knowing that there will be an ultimate and lasting dawn.

Individualization

As Christ, the Morning Star, illuminates our experience, He increasingly becomes our reality. But, for some, experiencing God in a progressive way is almost impossible because of the many layers of defense mechanisms making up their human construction. The voices of conscience, the past, and parental input, though they may be interpreted as God's voice, are only subjective echos reflecting one's yesterdays and the dominant influences of today. Relationships often substitute for relating to Christ. Relationships are sacred but in themselves are not our destiny. Believers must learn how to individualize because the partner, the friend, the association, and the pastor will not always be there. Individuals need to grow and change in their own personal destinies.

Christians stagnate because they do not adventure out of the old. Familiarity makes it difficult to experience the supernatural side of one's salvation. The negative frame of reference built over the years inhibits the soul from understanding hope. The natural man, "born unto trouble as the sparks fly upward," has difficulty comprehending what it means to have an All-Powerful God dwelling within.

Sin is natural but recovery is not. Recovery means being supernaturally restored to a supernatural walk. Mercy miraculously wipes away the scars of yesterday. "Be real" taunts the voice of a cursed creation. "Yes, be real," exclaims the indwelling Spirit: be real about your supernatural provision! Instead of looking to God first, we have been educated to do that which comes naturally first and if that fails, to look for supernatural help. Religion looks to human resources for reform and self-betterment. But God gives us a living hope. Free from our marriage to yesterday, we have a new Partner, Christ, who is in love with us whether we fail or succeed! This living relationship motivates us to look to Him, which causes us to become like Him in spite of ourselves!

Being accepted before change comes releases the soul to receive the power to change! God shakes our worlds and lets us fall so that we will forsake the old creation and live before Him, alone. Joshua stood in the

River Jordan until all the people passed over. Jesus stations Himself as our Mediator as we pass from death over to life in a process of faith. All the promises of Canaan are ours despite the giants still in the land, but we have to walk by faith in order to enter in. Every day we are getting closer to Christ, our hope of glory. Only pharisaical phonies profess that they never fail. Their religious defense mechanisms make them nonentities with God. But we can go beyond concepts and an unpurged conscience to grow into an eternal identity given by grace.

Christ is in the process of bringing many sons to glory. The treasure lies buried in the midst of a ruin—a history of sin, guilt, heartache, and pride. Outward rules can never substitute for an inward relationship which cleanses the soul from these points of reference. Each Christian is responsible for a direct vertical exchange with God. Sickness, accidents, and financial problems are all part of God's move to close in on us! Wilderness situations are ordained as times of facing God eyeball to eyeball. Naturally we react and look for a scapegoat. But we do not have to run. We can relax because God is in the driver's seat. It becomes easy when we give it all to Him, not even blaming ourselves.

Silver cannot be withdrawn from the fire until its Maker's reflection can be seen. Nothing will change or get better until we can reflect Christ in the midst of our situation. **That** is true progress. What we want and what we ought to be finally come together in the apprehension of God's love. No payment is being exacted but a substitutionary life is being offered. While it may seem hard to let go of the ego that has brought us thus far, our heavenly Bridegroom challenges every believer with this personal invitation: "It is the voice of my beloved that knocketh, saying, Open to Me... My love, My dove, My undefiled" (Song of Sol. 5:2).

Reflections

I thank God for the bitter things;
    They've been a "friend to grace";
They've driven me from the paths of ease
    To storm the secret place.

I thank Him for the friends who failed
    To fill my heart's deep need;
They've driven me to the Saviour's feet
    Upon His life to feed.

I'm grateful, too, through all life's way
    No one could satisfy,
And so I've found in God alone
    My rich, my full supply.

—Florence White Willett[1]

SEVEN

HUMAN RESPONSIBILITY

The growth process includes correction. Crisis smashes the shell of previously acquired subjective patterns so that we can enjoy the experience of our internal treasure. Chastening, as the normal interaction between parent and child, promotes continued and intensified fellowship in the new found relationship. Those who are "accepted in the Beloved" are accountable to all the privileges and responsibilities of their position. A dedicated monarch will discipline the heir apparent to the throne. "For whom the Lord loveth, He correcteth: even as a father the son in whom he delighteth" (Prov. 3:12). We have been made part of the royal family through the process of spiritual adoption. Just as my wife and I, many years ago, adopted a little five month old girl, God has adopted us as His legal heirs. As we grow up in Him, He watches over our development with a careful eye:

My son, do not make light of the Lord's discipline, and do not lose heart when He rebukes you, because the Lord disciplines those He loves and He punishes everyone He accepts as a son (Heb. 12:5-6; NIV).

In order for the Lord to effectively teach us, He must first cleanse the conscience. An adopted child who has experienced much previous abuse needs love and continual assurance of his new state before he can receive instruction without considering it rebuke or punishment. A Christian with an uncleansed conscience always thinks God is punishing when anything remotely negative happens. "Perfect love casts out fear" (1 John 4:18). A healthy fear of the Lord is based on absolute trust in His loving character and resulting reverence for all His ways.

RSVP

Most invitations include an RSVP, the abbreviated form of the French phrase "please respond!" Every one of God's promises which invite us to partake of His nature bear an invisible RSVP. Divine grace does not bypass human participation. Salvation without obedience is profession without possession. The experience of grace is reserved for those who humble themselves to respond. Free volition must reckon on God's Word in order to release its power. That is why faith is referred to as a "work" in John, chapter six and Hebrews, chapter four. Passivity is not the same as faith-rest. One is the paralyzing effect of unbelief and the other is the release that comes from reliance on Christ's completed work.

True repentance is the soul cooperating with the gift of grace; it is the effect of the gospel on the responsive human heart. It is God's will that we experience an ongoing repentance through the continual transformation of the mind. Faith comes by hearing the Word of God which is a critic and accurate judge of the heart. God's Word separates the old lines of the fallen mind from the fresh perspective of the Holy Spirit. The Apostle Paul said, "I commend you to God, and to the word of His grace, which is able to build you up, and to give you an inheritance among all them which are sanctified" (Acts 20:32).

It is not the dead letter which converts the soul but the living sword of the Spirit which releases the human psyche and will. "The letter killeth" (2 Cor. 3:6). Those who try to chasten their own soul with verses of condemnation only strengthen their own weaknesses. That is why a skilled pastor-teacher is imperative for the Christian who desires to really grow under God's instruction. The workman trained in the Word is able to rightly divide truth so the flesh is bound and the spirit is released, not vice versa! Under the discipline of academic learning, a transforming process occurs as the downward pull of the fall is neutralized and the spiritual man is quickened. "Where the Spirit of the Lord is, there is liberty. But we all, with open face beholding as in a glass the glory of the Lord, are changed into the same image from glory to glory, even as by the Spirit of the Lord" (2 Cor. 3:17-18). The glass is the Word of God. The veil of the Law strengthening the inability of the flesh has been removed. The glory of the Lord is the revelation of grace through Calvary. That is what changes an individual!

Esau repented but he never changed because he rejected his birthright. Some Christians reject their new identity through the new birth by continually trying to change what God has and is changing. The activity of their will is actually counter-productive. Tears are shed and efforts made again and again without lasting effects because of the wrong premise for repentance. "Works meet for repentance" speaks of having active and absolute faith in the Son's forgiving power. Repentance does not mean demonstrating outward proof of being sorry so that one can be restored. There is no such thing as "easy believism." There is only one kind of true believism and that is in the work and person of Jesus Christ. "Abraham believed God, and it was counted unto him for righteousness" (Rom. 4:3).

Faith frees the soul from guilt and striving so that it can function in the Spirit. The fruits of functioning in the Spirit are love, joy, peace, longsuffering, gentleness, goodness, faith, meekness, and temperance—"against such there is no law" (Gal. 5:22-23). God's Word will produce the fruit if we do our part which is to believe. Just as looking to the brazen serpent in Numbers 21 healed the people of their serpent bites, we experience progressive healing by gazing on Christ through the Word. "Whereby are given unto us exceeding great and precious promises: that by these ye might be partakers of the divine nature, having escaped the corruption that is in the world through lust" (2 Pet. 1:4). When we look at God's promises through the eye of faith, everything else about our lives begins to reflect His goodness. "The light of the body is the eye: if therefore thine eye be single, thy whole body shall be full of light" (Matt. 6:22). The Word of God lights our path so that we can hear the voice of the Spirit saying "This is the way, walk ye in it" (Isa. 30:21). Therefore, the Bible, communicated in life, is God's desired means of instruction and correction.

Godly Sorrow

When Isaiah saw the Lord high and lifted up in His finished work position, he cried: "Woe is me! for I am undone; because I am a man of unclean lips, and I dwell in the midst of a people of unclean lips: for mine eyes have seen the king, the Lord of hosts" (Isa. 6:5). The revelation of God is always accompanied by the consciousness of having fallen short of His glory. Peter cried "depart from me; for I am a sinful man, O Lord" when He realized who Jesus really was. Conviction (not condemnation) is the response of the soul to God's Presence. Because God is invisible, believers can easily become familiar with what they think they know about Him and live by knowledge instead of communion. Isaiah was shocked to realize that he had not been speaking from the throne so the people had been left unchanged.

The Word of God, properly expressed through the Spirit, rouses us out of our natural complacency with self and our tolerance of sin. The apostle Paul shook up the Corinthians when he wrote to them. His words caused sorrow when they realized they had not handled a specific situation in the church with Christ's mind. They were sorry because they really loved God and loved Paul. Their sorrow led to instant obedience. Worldly sorrow is being sorry for getting caught and having to bear the consequences. Godly sorrow means being heartbroken because of love. God's power does all the changing but we walk sensitively and reverently because it is God's power. Brokenness which leads to obedience is the full manifestation of the true heart of faith.

Sensitivity to the probings of the Holy Spirit through God's Word will keep us spiritually up to date in a continual cleansing process. The same responsive capacity which said "yes" to the invitation of salvation, continues to receive power to become a prayer warrior, a church member, and a soul winner.

The Contrite Heart

There is a holy sacrifice
which God in heaven will not despise
Yea, which is precious in His eyes—
> The contrite heart.

The Holy One, the Son of God
His pardoning love will shed abroad,
And consecrate as His abode—
> The contrite heart.

The Holy Spirit from on high
will listen to its faintest sigh,
And cheer and bless and purify
> The contrite heart.

Saviour, I cast my hopes on Thee;
such as Thou art, I fain would be!
In mercy, Lord, bestow on me
> The contrite heart.
> > —Montgomery[1]

Meekness leads to motivation. Looking unto Jesus provides the impetus to run the race. Exhaustion (because of procrastination), and distraction (because of self-occupation) are the twin enemies which cause us to neglect cultivating our responsive capacity toward grace to be made like Christ through the Spirit.

We should never underestimate the ability of God's Word to convict and convert its listener. Recently a Bible College student was witnessing to a man in the inner city. The man looked at him and said, "you have ruined my evening." It turned out he had been in the streets for the purpose of robbing someone that evening, but the student's words changed his mind and the would-be robber gave his heart to Jesus instead! Zaccheus, the public menace, becomes Zaccheus, the public benefactor after being in the Master's Presence! What the law could never do, grace is able to accomplish within the heart of one who lets God in.

God's Order

Order preserves our freedom to grow and develop. Order in the church keeps the devil and confusion out. Every institution must have order in order to function. A person on an independent ego trip may accuse a ministry of being legalistic when it is only being orderly. God has ordained authority for man's protection. "For rulers are not a terror to good works, but to the evil" (Rom. 13:3). Proper delegated authority in the church is given for the believers' edification, not their destruction. The overseeing pastor is commanded by God to preach, reprove and rebuke, giving God's Word and Spirit free sway in hearts and lives. National order protects the functioning of the church. Ministerial order protects the functioning of the individual. Personal order releases the free functioning of the Word and Spirit within.

In Ephesians 4:11, the gifts which Christ bestows on the church are people ordained to lead it into fruitful production. Honoring the table of organization enables productivity in the plan of God. A chain of command is necessary because of the devil's continued presence in this world. Directly after the fall, Adam was put in charge as Eve's head so that she would be protected from demonic influence. Humility in the local assembly provides spiritual protection: "Because your adversary the devil, as a roaring lion, walketh about, seeking whom he may devour" (1 Pet. 5:8).

To keep out this master of confusion, there is an order that we must follow if a brother sins. By following this order, his freedom to grow is preserved and the integrity of the entire church is maintained. Just after Jesus spoke of protecting God's little ones and of the Shepherd's heart to retrieve the one little lamb gone astray, He gave these instructions concerning the order of restoration which the church was to practice: "If thy brother shall trespass against thee" [notice, the trespass must be against **you**, personally. If it does not involve you, you are to keep out of it because it is none of your concern!], "go and tell him his fault between thee and him alone: if he shall hear thee, thou has gained thy brother. But if he will not hear thee, then take with thee one or two more, that in the mouth of two or three witnesses every word may be established. And if he shall neglect to hear the church: let him be unto thee as an heathen man and a publican" (Matt. 18:15-17).

The motive for confronting a brother is to win him back into fellowship with the truth. Sin does not make him lose his status as a brother. Family signifies a blood-tie which can never be denied. Every believer has been washed by the same blood and is part of the family of God forever. If the fallen brother responds to the initiations of love and he repents, the matter is finished. It is forgiven, forgotten and over. It cannot be brought up again at a later date as spiritual blackmail. It is not God's will that we live in constant fear of being exposed for past failures. Those who are truly spiritual seek to reconcile and restore, not expose and defeat.

"Brethren, if a man be overtaken in a fault, ye which are spiritual, restore such an one in the spirit of meekness; considering thyself, lest thou also be tempted" (Gal. 6:1). The Greek word for "restore" was also often used in reference to mending nets. The body of Christ is the net with which we catch men. Hearts must be mended and restored in order for the church to properly function. Another meaning of "restore" is to set back in place a dislocated joint. The backslider is a dislocated, not a severed, member who has been distracted from his position in Christ because of a hard tackle. Christians who have sinned have been knocked down by temptation. They are disjointed, in need of mending and loving restoration.

"Redeeming the time," in regard to one who sins, means to make every effort to restore a brother as soon as possible. A young person who falls into immorality at sixteen should not have to spend several years of his life in guilt, sorrow and isolation. He needs to be forgiven, restored, loved. There are many productive years left to his life and we can be the means of redeeming those years. Husbands and wives can redeem the time in marriage by not letting petty arguments be blown out of proportion. The rising divorce rate among Christian couples is a symptom of progressive hard-heartedness and a lack of understanding biblical reconciliation.

The case in the Corinthian church of the man who was living in open adultery with his stepmother was dealt with immediately upon reception of Paul's orders. Because he refused to repent, the whole church agreed to treat him as a heathen and not fellowship with him. Brokenhearted, the man forsook his sin because the pleasures of the flesh can never substitute for the joys of spiritual communion. Like one preacher said, "The first day of sin is the best day because after that, the guilt and bondage only grow worse and worse." Unfortunately, this repentant brother was not restored as immediately as he was formerly ostracized. Paul had to write another letter of instruction telling the church to receive him back into fellowship because he had forsaken his sin.

God's heart is to leave the ninety and nine and to restore the one who has fallen. It is not the office of the church to teach the fallen one a lesson. "Thine own wickedness shall correct thee, and thy backslidings shall reprove thee" (Jer. 2:19). Sin, itself, is the best incentive not to do it again.

Failure is a better teacher than success
But she seldom finds an apple on her desk!

Righteous Judgment

Human responsibility requires the Christian to make proper kinds of judgments as he interacts with those in his sphere. The Apostle Paul scolded the Corinthians for not judging the case of open adultery. The local assembly has the right and the duty to make value judgments concerning anything which affects the welfare of its membership. Paul instructed his flock not to eat with any church member who was living in open opposition to the character of God. Not only was immorality an issue, but also gossip, criticism, extortion and drunkenness. Paul recommended this isolation policy, not because of hate but because of love. Love for God, love for purity, love for the church and love for the backslidden church member constrains the discerning Christian to take uncompromising action. In 1 Corinthians 11:22-31, many were sick, and some even died in the church for not discerning the body of Christ when they partook of communion. They suffered because of not rightly judging!

The Apostle Peter held Ananias and Sapphira responsible for the lie they told about the value of the property which they had sold and donated to the church. The consequences of their sin shocked the entire congregation! Bona fide judgment protects the whole church. The table of organization must be honored whether it is in the home, an athletic association, or a business; but especially in the church which should represent the mind of Christ. Paul appeared before the church council in Acts 15:4. He submitted himself to proper procedures, trusting the elders' powers of discernment. In 1 Corinthians 6, Paul recommends that the church settle disputes between its members instead of having them tried before the eyes of the world in the secular court system. His reasoning was that since the saints are going to one day judge the spirit world with Christ, they should be able to settle smaller, earthly matters!

In Acts 17:11, the Bereans were commended for using their faculties, researching the Scriptures to rightly judge Paul's message. "Strong meat belongeth to them that are of full age, even those who by reason of use have their senses exercised to discern both good and evil" (Heb. 5:14). In looking for a church and spiritual fellowship, discernment is imperative. "Beloved, believe not every spirit, but try the spirits whether they are of God" (1 John 4:1). Any teacher or preacher who denies the incarnation is not of God and must be considered a false prophet. False churches have every liberty to exist and true Christians have every liberty to discern and avoid them. We are commanded to test, to prove and to scrutinize the doctrine of a church before we join it to see if they believe in the deity of Christ and the cardinal doctrines of faith.

Christ needs His disciples to discern between the better and the best, as well. He does not want us to simply settle for something good. He has a perfect will and plan for each life. In Romans 4:20, Abraham studied the promise of God all the way through to its logical end. He rightly judged the character of the Promiser, making his decisions based upon that judgment.

In James, chapter three, we are to judge ourselves by what comes out of our mouths! True wisdom manifests itself in purity and peaceableness. "Judge not according to the appearance, but judge righteous judgment" (John 7:24). Carnal judgment is based upon sight and hearsay. We are not to make judgments of comparison between servants of Christ, quibble over lesser doctrines, interpretations and preferences, or condemn ourselves if we are living up to the truth that we have been taught. We are not to judge those not in our jurisdiction. If the trespass in question involves the assembly that I am in, I have every right to inform the pastor so that a little leaven does not affect the whole. But if it does not concern me or my church, I have no right to become involved in the judging process. Thousands of Christians have transgressed in this area simply by reading the newspaper!

> They search out iniquities; they accomplish a diligent search: both the inward thought of every one of them, and the heart, is deep. But God shall shoot at them with an arrow; sud-

denly shall they be wounded. So they shall
make their own tongue to fall upon themselves: all that see them shall flee away (Ps.
64:6-8).

According to 1 Corinthians 4:5, we cannot judge
men's motives. Since we are all in the process of growth,
we cannot always discern people's hearts by their actions.
They may be failing miserably outwardly but growing
inwardly. We cannot judge one another's convictions.
Each must be allowed to live unto the Lord. Destructive
criticism, personal crusades against other churches, vin-
dictiveness and reactionary campaigns are all condemned
by the Word of God.

EIGHT

CAPITALIZING ON FAILURE

Today's coliseum mentality thrives on putting on trial before the lions men and women who profess to have faith. The public sits in the grandstands of human evaluation hoping fallen heros will "get theirs" for the very failures which characterize their own lives. There is a thirst for blood in the air. Why are so many ready to assume the worst and so few disposed to believe the best? A lynch-mob mentality is forming, with well-known Christian leaders in the fore. Instead of preaching the gospel, these men seem to be elevating themselves upon the failures of others.

Failure can be a pedestal for the light, if Christ is magnified in the midst. But instead of lifting up the Light of the world, light is being obscured by pointing fingers and eager voices coming forward with the "evidence." This is not a climate conducive to honest growth, emotional healing, or promotion of the glad tidings of God's forgiveness through Christ.

Recently, news of the failure of a well-known minister was the headline story in newspapers and on television. A number of other Christian ministers collaborated with the secular media to circulate details and allegations concerning this man's life. These Christian leaders collaborated with the world and even commended the media for its coverage of the story. Are these men ignorant of the apostle Paul's words in 2 Corinthians 6:14-15? "Be not unequally yoked together with unbelievers: for what fellowship hath righteousness with unrighteousness? And what communion hath light with darkness? And what concord hath Christ with Belial? Or what part hath he that believeth with an infidel?"

In this situation, believers of the light joined forces with those of the darkness. What was the effect? The entire evangelical Christian community was placed under suspicion. As one pastor said, "It was a tremendous blow to the cause of Christ as a whole." These Christian leaders did the world a favor, not the Church. The damage they inflicted may take years to heal. Furthermore, should they be caught in a similar failure, the same media that listened so respectfully to them and published their comments will turn its focus on them.

This is not to excuse the man's sin. He is a public figure and is paying a severe price for his wrong decisions. He is accountable to his local church and to the organization that sanctioned him as a minister. However, any matter involving a believer who personally sins but does not break any civil laws should be handled in proper scriptural order within these structures. He remains a member of the body of Christ. He needed and still needs

Christ's love.

There is a growing social mind-set against evangelical Christianity which makes failure a matter of public rejoicing. When we consider the Jonestown tragedy of 1978, we are reminded of the Christians being implicated in the burning of Rome! The "Reverend" Jim Jones established a quasi-Christian community in the jungle of Guyana with no church, no chapel, and no place of prayer. Jones, explicitly socialistic, at the time of his death was reportedly negotiating with the Soviet Union for a new home of his "experiment in socialism." Ignoring the overwhelming evidence of the political nature of the organization, public consensus has made "religious fanaticism" the focus of this world-renowned scandal.

Right up until the time a bullet hit his leg, a visiting eye witness of the *Washington Post* was planning to write an admiring article of Jonestown's ideals which, as he saw it, had all the essentials of progressive politics. Its doctrine was social change; its catechism, radical politics. Jones was a Marxist who called the Bible "a paper idol" but when his experiment ended in terror, the Bible and those who adhere to it took the rap.

A zealous determination to "save" unwitting victims has turned a savage public on an unsuspecting Church. It is with a self-justifying sense of conscience that accusations are now being fielded and launched across the newspapers, courts and conversations of the country concerning the danger of religion that "hoodwinks the masses."

"Scaring Up Business"

A multimillion dollar business has been contributing to the public paranoia concerning religion. In 1974

Ted Patrick, convicted felon and father of the practice of forcible abduction and faithbreaking, founded an organization dedicated to "deprogramming" young adults who join religious groups against parental wishes. The Cult Awareness Network has grown out of his philosophy of spreading mass hysteria under a cleverly concealed hate campaign. This well-funded witch-hunting crusade has succeeded in turning Lutherans against Pentecostals, Catholics against Protestants, and Jews against Evangelicals.

In an attempt to intensify fear and suspicion, Billy Graham's name is being linked with Yogi Bhajan's and Campus Crusade with Hare Krishna! Although CAN's methodology of deprogramming has been publicly condemned by nearly every religious organization in America (The National Council of Churches, the Baptist Joint Committee, the United States Catholic Conference, the National Association of Evangelicals, the Lutheran Council in the USA, and the Synagogue Council of America, as well as the American Civil Liberties Union all thoroughly condemn the practice), many churches in these denominations continue to promote their anti-religious material, and church members pay thousands of dollars to "rescue" their own from the church down the street.

Competition is certainly motivating the support behind the "liberation" of loved ones from a chosen religious affiliation. During the 1960s and 70s, mainline churches lost a large potential membership among their young adults. At the same time, fundamentalist and evangelical churches boomed as tens of millions of Americans declared themselves to be born-again. It was in reaction to these departures from traditional religion that the propaganda campaigns began. It is an old story, but one that could have unforeseen repercussions if played out in modern times.

It is ironic that the very churches who were once grossly mistreated themselves are now the self-deputized vigilantes of the so-called "anti-cult" movement. (By the way, Reinhard Heydrich, infamous for his authority over the first few months of the murder of the European Jews, just previously had been given the assignment of ridding the German Reich of its "cults and sects.") At one time, Catholics experienced some of the most severe discrimination and violent persecution in American history. With the influx of Irish immigrants in the 1820s and 30s, Protestants felt their religion and communities defied Anglo-American conformity. Their private schools and campaigns to convert Protestants were viewed as subversive. Horror stories circulated about cultic convents and power-mad priests which remarkably parallel the controversy targeting independent churches today. Deception, coercion, perversion, subversion, mind control, and exploitation were the indictments leveled against them. Ex-members who "escaped" to tell their lurid stories were often discovered to have private motives for joining the ranks of the opponents. Many of their testimonies were ghost-written by leaders of the anti-Catholic movement (read *Strange Gods* by David G. Bromley). Perhaps Protestantism was only having its revenge on the ravaged reputation of John Calvin who was "exposed" by a Carmelite who had been temporarily converted to evangelicalism. He accused Calvin of being an impostor—who claimed he could resurrect the dead, and a sodomite who had been sentenced to be branded with a red-hot iron!

As this replay of the war between the ecclesiastical

empires rages, everyone involved is getting hurt. Those in churches are wounded by becoming involved in reactionary endeavors instead of concentrating on God's healing love, and spectators outside of the church grow more convinced than ever that "churchianity" is only a power play and nothing more. As one man quipped, "Doctors tell us that hating people can cause cancer, heart attacks, headaches, skin rashes, and asthma. It doesn't make the people we hate feel too good either!"

The alarming reality concerning these denominational war games is the effect they are having on national religious freedoms. A pervasively negative image of grassroots Christianity has spread a popular public prejudice against any religious belief which goes beyond the nominal to occupy a dominant place in daily life.

The Failure Hype

A viper bit a slanderer in the side;
The slanderer lived, but the viper died![1]

The same press which taught the American public to hate the Shah of Iran, portrayed Koemini as a benevolent representative of the people. Yet Koemini killed more people in a twenty hour period than the Shah had killed in twenty years! Headlines are often only publicly-sanctioned slander. Abraham Lincoln said that if he read all the criticisms directed at him, he would have time for nothing else! Once alerted to the popular cult issue, the media has been quick to seize upon sensational stories of impropriety, financial misappropriation, and the like. Everybody wants to hear the truth—especially about somebody else!

Slanted reporting and conviction by innuendo has

been decried by thousands of clergy and ministries across our land. Derogatory stories are being printed without thorough investigation of the facts and which make no attempt to present a balanced picture. Wild accusations make good copy, increasing newspaper circulation and station appeal. These days the story of a preacher accused of wrongdoing is just too juicy to pass up! Many of the "witnesses" providing the material later confess their lies once the damage already has been done. Twelve thousand court cases against churches were reported in 1988, and we can be sure that each of them had to battle a full scale war involving media-distorted information negatively influencing the public. Elmer Gantry and Marjoe-type imaging has brought ridicule on the servants of Christ, as well as material loss.

There is an audience for a complaint against a church. Recently, a Franciscan priest who runs a mission in New York City was accused of sexual and financial wrongdoing. The accuser's father was flown in to testify that his son was a chronic liar with a personality disorder, who was driven to hurt everyone who tried to help him. The accusations had no validity but they were made during a peak fund-raising period at Christmas. Many in the congregation were angered and saddened by the way the media handled the case. Their spokesman said, "It's turning out to be the classic story of a mentally unstable person who was able to use the worst example of tabloid journalism."

The tragedy is that this incident is not isolated, but typical. The image-making power of the media extends into every arena. The editor-in-chief of *U.S. News and World Report* began a recent article this way: "The American people are being brainwashed. It has been a long and subtle process, principally through the medium of television." He was addressing the public mood which was being conditioned to accept measures which would jeopardize the national security of Israel. He did not see the process as a deliberate plot, but a result of the veneration of action news which inflames the emotions while taking little time to research context, history, and character.

To quote Francis Schaeffer, "The media and especially television have indeed changed the perception of not only current events, but also of the political process. They are so powerful that they act as if they were the fourth branch of government in the United States. Their ability to change our perception of any event raises serious questions concerning the democratic process. Christians must certainly not uncritically accept what they read, and especially what they see on television, as objective."

We are at the capricious mercy of popular sentiment. Whether we will be represented as villains or heros depends upon the prejudice currently in vogue. David Livingstone, once hailed as an unrivaled explorer and medical missionary, revered as a near saint who epitomized every moral virtue, in latter times was "unmasked" as an arrogant interferer who wantonly enforced alien and unsuitable values on innocent and ideal societies! In all reality, he was neither model of perfection nor culture wrecker. He was a man with a dream, a human being with many failures who succeeded by daring to advance into pioneer territory led by biblical convictions. Society once revered such individuals but the pendulum is swinging the other way as the sacred is being connected with scandal and we face a new kind of inquisition.

Indeed, as an article in the *Annals of America* points

out, had Abraham been alive today, he would have been charged with attempted murder for his faith on Mt. Moriah. Moses would have been billed as a charismatic leader drawing thousands of gullible followers to mass starvation in the wilderness. Jesus would certainly have been (as he was then) arraigned as a public threat for His wild assertions of His coming kingdom.

The Lie

First somebody told it, then the room couldn't
  hold it,
So the busy tongues rolled it 'til they got it
  outside.
Then the crowd came across it, and never once
  lost it,
But tossed it and tossed it, 'til it grew long and
  wide.

This lie brought forth others, both sisters and
  brothers,
And fathers and mothers—a terrible crew.
And while headlong they hurried, the people
  they flurried,
And troubled and worried, as lies always do.

And so evil-bodied, this monster lay goaded
'Til at last it exploded in smoke and in shame.
Then from mud and from mire, the pieces flew
  higher
And hit the sad liar and killed a good name.
  —Anonymous

When a prominent Christian figure is accused of failure, where are the other well-known Christians who should be standing by his side? They are hiding behind enemy fire, secretly rejoicing in their brother's downfall and waiting for their turn to be called forward to denounce the fallen one. It is too reminiscent of scenes recorded by Christians under repressive socialist control.

"A brother is born for adversity" (Prov. 17:17). When Saul lost his battle and the enemies rejoiced, David put aside his personal conflict with him to defend Saul's name. "Publish it not in Gath!" he cried. No matter what internal fighting transpired, David was anxious to present a unified front of their mutual cause.

When Noah, father, preacher, and government leader, was discovered naked in a drunken condition, Ham—his own son—exposed him to public ridicule. The man who went on a "save the world" campaign was found in a state of debauchery! Surely this was headline material! Ham's two other brothers, honoring their father's position, walked backwards into Noah's tent carrying a blanket with which to cover him. They would have no eye-witness testimony to give.

The Church is being lured into the world via the microphone, television camera, and witness stand to disown its own. Is this real integrity? The Bible tells us that Ham was cursed and his brethren blessed as a result of their response to the situation. A real Christian is as horrified by his own sins as he is by his neighbor's! Erwin W. Lutzer accurately sums up the paranoia that often prevents Christians from standing by those who have lost public face: "Befriending the fallen does appear to be taking a soft approach to sin. If a man sins, he ought to pay for it; if he is restored too easily, we are giving the impression that sin is not that serious. So we justify our inaction with the belief that the offender is just getting his due. Second, we may even be afraid of guilt by association. If we are known to be spending time with one who failed, we may be considered by others as being guilty, too. Birds of a feather flock together!"[2]

In the middle of Deborah's triumphant song of praise for a mighty victory, the angel of the Lord interjected a curse against the inhabitants of Meroz "because they came not to the help of the Lord." Jesus asked Saul of Tarsus, "Why persecutest thou Me?" when Saul was accusing and bringing to trial the early Christians. Christ ever identifies with the hurts of His people. He says, "Inasmuch as ye have done it unto one of the least of these My brethren, ye have done it unto Me" (Matt. 25:40). The sins of omission being judged in that text were those towards the downcast and outcast: "...naked and ye clothed Me not, sick and in prison and ye visited Me not." What were they in prison for? Surely, if someone has done wrong, we must not identify with them! The lack of compassion, identification, and fidelity under pressure among the brethren has contributed to the disintegration of the image of the Church at large and the disorientation of its membership. Speaking engagements are broken, long-standing friendships severed, and God's blessings withheld because no one wants to be associated with the "failure" of a brother who is guilty until proven innocent.

How tenderly I cherish the memory of a dear Catholic brother in New England, Ed Massery, now gone home to be with the Lord. In the face of public censure and town gossip, he extended a firm hand of fellowship to me and my church at that time. He was not afraid to get involved. He shared prayer and pulpit, always edifying me behind my back and actively identifying with the cause of Christ.

Prominent church leaders who take turns criticizing each other before the public eye should take heed to Romans 14:4: "Who art thou that judgest another man's servant? To his own Master he standeth or falleth. Yea, he shall be holden up: for God is able to make him stand." Whether it is concerning doctrinal disputations, organizational differences, or reports of wrongdoing, we are to honor the stewardship of grace, especially before the unbelieving. Nathan reproved David, saying "By this deed thou hast given great occasion to the enemies of the Lord to blaspheme" (2 Sam. 12:14). The world is capitalizing on reports of failure. We do not need to help them!

Judge Not

Judge not!—though clouds of seeming guilt
    may dim thy brother's fame;
For fate may throw suspicion's shade upon the
    brightest name;
Thou canst not tell what hidden chain of
    circumstances may
Have wrought the sad result that takes an
    honest name away.
        Judge not!

Judge not!—the vilest criminal may rightfully
    demand
A chance to prove his innocence by jury of his
    land;
And, surely, one who ne'er was known to break
    his plighted word,
Should not be hastily condemned to obloquy
    unheard.
        Judge not!

Judge not!—thou canst not tell how soon the
    look of bitter scorn
May rest on thee, though pure thy heart as dew-
    drops in the morn.
Thou dost not know what freak of fate may
    place upon thy brow
A cloud of shame to kill the joy that rests upon
    it now.
            Judge not!

Judge not!—but rather in thy heart let gentle
    pity dwell;
Man's judgment errs, but there is One who
    "doeth all things well."
Ever, throughout the voyage of life, this
    precept keep in view:
"Do unto others as thou wouldst that they
    should do to you."
            Judge not!

Judge not!—for one unjust reproach an honest
    heart can feel
As keenly as the deadly stab made by the
    pointed steel.
The worm will kill the sturdy oak, though
    slowly it may die,
As surely as the lightning stroke swift rushing
    from the sky.
            Judge not!
               —Anonymous

A Greater Failure

What freedoms are at risk while Christians fail each

other and the media spotlights the process? Donald Sills, president of the Coalition for Religious Freedom, a Baptist preacher for 25 years, believes the anti-Christian movement in this country operating under the guise of cult control could potentially have the power of regulating all religious groups.

A new anti-cult forum in the form of hearings on the Guayana tragedy was formed in the Senate, serving as a catalyst to the formation of the American Family Foundation, a private interest hate group. Dr. John Clark, a psychiatrist serving this organization, was reprimanded by his peers after he falsely claimed to be conducting an official study on "mind control" for the Massachusetts General Hospital while, in reality, pursuing his anti-cult activities. He had been reprimanded earlier by the Commonwealth of Massachusetts Board of Registration and Discipline in Medicine for committing an individual to a psychiatric hospital without an examination. The chief aim of these groups is to push federal legislation that would make "mind control" a felony and require existing "cult" members to submit to physical and mental examination by non-cult physicians.

Reverend James Bevel, leader of the Selma Right to Vote Movement, cites such thinking as typical of minority hate groups. "If we study the demeanor, attitudes, expressions, and intensity in the Cult Awareness people, we would see that it is identical to the demeanor, attitudes, and expressions of the Klu Klux Klan." Reverend Jim Nicholls of the Assemblies of God notes their motives as being "out for the money and/or the destruction of religion, itself."

A pseudo-concern for mental health ignores the spiritual aspect of personhood, making anyone propagating a spiritual product suspect. By taking advantage of scandalous stories and preying on public fears, they are bringing the very plausibility of authentic conversion into question. Anti-religious legislation would pose a threat to the pluralistic character of American society and reveal the very propensity toward totalitarianism which such legislation would be trying to prevent.

How far has this anti-religious movement progressed? Among the notable church-state cases of 1989 was the ruling made by a federal judge that a Denver teacher did not have the right to have books on Christianity in his classroom library, or to read the Bible silently during classroom hours! In another case, based upon the accusation of excessive child abuse made by an ex-member against a community church, the State of Vermont conducted a massive raid and took all of the children of the group into custody. Two months after the raid, the ex-member confessed that he lied in making the charges in order to justify his departure from the congregation.

The fundamentalist mind-set is being perceived as "a psychological...social disease," to quote an anti-fundamentalist propaganda sheet. Says David Rodier, professor of religion at American University: "They're branding groups and individuals who believe in evangelism. I don't see what's left of Christianity if you forbid evangelistic efforts." Biblical aspects of Christian life such as witnessing, spiritual leadership, conversion, reproof, correction, and Bible teaching are being labeled as recruiting, shepherding, indoctrination, mind control and brainwashing.

According to *The Christian Cause* (1987), those seeking control and the right to decide what is "good" religion are being given respect and credibility by an increasing number of lawyers, judges, and legislators in a direct frontal attack on the First Amendment right to free exercise of religion. "Legislators will listen to us and work around every First Amendment obstruction if they know we are strong enough to vote them out of office," confidently exulted John Sweeney, former executive director of CAN. The type of legislation that has been suggested includes curbs on evangelism requiring evangelists to obtain licenses, the lifting of tax-exemptions, and court-ordered psychiatry for converts.

In 1987, it was estimated that forty times a week, nationwide, adult men and women were held against their will, forced to read literature and watch films attacking the victim's religious group. Dr. Gordon Melton, Methodist minister and author, comments, "a massive assault upon the psyche and value system of the victim is as traumatic for some as a physical rape. If the deprogramming victim attempts resistance and escape, she or he will almost surely be physically assaulted and often restrained with ropes and/or handcuffs. On several occasions deprogramming of female victims has led to sexual assault. In one case, the husband of a woman undergoing deprogramming was severely cut with a razor while trying to free his wife from her abductors." Some have reported being kicked, thrown against walls, and beaten. Clothes have been ripped off, ice applied night and day, and sleep deprived in these dehumanizing practices.

These concentration camp tactics are employed by "exit counselors" earning $15-40,000 per case who have no authorized training and often cause irreversible damage in familial relationships. After they persuade the person to leave their religious affiliation, they can turn around and sue the church, with the lawyers getting 50% of the damages! Organizations promoting these faith-breaking sessions have a national network and have even attempted to gain medical approval in order to legitimize their activities enough so that Blue Cross would pick up the bulk of the tab!

Many parents and deprogrammers have escaped conviction because the police or prosecutors looked the other way, or have been acquitted under the plea "necessity of defense." They rationalize that the end justifies the means, although this is one of the primary "doctrines" which they accuse dictatorial religious groups of using.

Estimates from the Friends of Freedom research files indicate that more than half of the membership of the Cult Awareness Network is actively engaged in some phase of the kidnapping, transportation, psychological indoctrination, legal protection, or staffing of hidden retreat centers or other support for deprogramming acts. The Reverend Dean Kelly, Director of civil and religious liberty for the National Council of Churches, says that "forcible deprogramming is the most serious stain on religious liberty facing this country in the later half of the 20th century."

Some say this attack on fundamentalism is a smoke screen to discredit those with whom they disagree politically. They believe the movement is part of a reactionary response to the growing number of Christians who are becoming involved in the political process.

Harvey Cox, Thomas Professor of Divinity at Harvard University, says that the word "cult" has become a term used to refer to any religious movement one does not like. He observes, "There are certainly dishonest and scheming individuals operating in religious movements and in many other kinds of movements as well. The 'cult scare,' however, goes far beyond any legitimate cause for concern. It conjures up a general specter, a Godzilla from the depths that must be destroyed by any means available. The fact is, however, that legislation already exists to countermand all the illegal acts attributed to the religious movements and leaders who violate such laws. No advocate of religious freedom defends the right of someone to deprive people of their freedom or to falsify income taxes just because he or she is a religious leader. Being a religious leader does not exempt anyone from criminal liability." He goes on to say that "those who have created the great cult scare are not satisfied with these forms of protection and refutation. They want to marshal the power of the State, the churches, the mental health profession, and other sectors of the society in rooting out something they see as an unprecedented threat, and they are perfectly willing to sacrifice legal guarantees, established scholarly procedures, and accepted boundaries of civil discourse to do so. If there is a menace abroad, it is probably the growing power of the alliance between government and mental health sectors to keep people thinking and acting the way those in charge think they should."[3]

1991 heralds the 200th birthday of the Bill of Rights. Religious freedom has been under stronger assault during the last decade than in any other period in our nation's history. Since 1980, there have been more court cases involving religious liberty than the total number during the previous 190 years! The preservation of our rights guaranteed under the Constitution of the United States must be upheld at any and all cost.

Let us not be intimidated in the face of accelerated public misunderstanding of "authentic" religious behavior by implications of fanaticism. An old church publication reports an incident of an officer complaining to General Stonewall Jackson that some soldiers were making noise in their tent. "What are they doing?" asked the General. "They are praying now, but they have been singing" was the reply. "And is that a crime?" the General demanded. "The articles of war orders punishment for an unusual noise" came the answer. "God forbid that praying should be an unusual noise in the camp" replied General Jackson.

Revival is atypical and not the accepted norm in any time period. G. Campbell Morgan heard this statement made: "The preacher must catch the spirit of the age." He gave the following answer: "God forgive him if he does. The preacher's business is to correct the spirit of the age!" Neither the Church in the Book of Acts nor the church of Philadelphia in Revelation were popular with the status quo. "Where there's smoke, there's fire"—Christians on fire for God! The only way to ascertain if a ministry is of God is to search the Scriptures to test their doctrine, and to personally inspect the fruit of their lives.

Hearsay and popular reports of wrongdoing characterize a post-Christian era that has forgotten the Christ of the Bible who said: "Woe unto you when all men shall speak well of you! for so did their fathers of the false prophets... Blessed are ye, when men shall revile you, and persecute you, and shall say all manner of evil against you falsely, for My sake. Rejoice and be exceeding glad!" (Luke 6:26; Matt. 5:11-12).

God Give Us Men

God give us men. A time like this demands
Strong minds, great hearts, true faith and
    willing hands;
Men whom the lust of office does not kill;
Men whom the spoils of office cannot buy;
Men who possess opinions and a will;
Men who have honor; men who will not lie;
Men who can stand before a demagogue
And damn his treacherous flatteries without
    winking;
Tall men, sun-crowned, who live above the fog
In public duty and in private thinking!
For while the rabble with their thumb-worn
    creeds,
Their large professions and their little deeds
Mingle in selfish strife; lo! Freedom weeps!
Wrong rules the land, and waiting Justice sleeps!
            —J. G. Holland

NINE

THE SPIRIT OF THE CHURCH

When the Apostle Paul told the Corinthians to examine their faith, he was writing to a church who had been cross-examining him! They were split into factions because they would not agree on whom to follow. The most arrogant party among them was the group for whom no human leader was good enough. They claimed God, alone, was their teacher.

Congregations have a way of putting all the blame on the pastor. Recent failures in church leadership which have been widely publicized have added to the board members' zeal to carve the splinter out of the preacher's eye! R. Eugene Puckett, editor-in-chief of a North Carolina Baptist newspaper, comments "We've been infiltrated with secular values in the church. In the secular world, a man produces or you chop off his head." It is common practice in churches across the country to terminate ministers after only five years of service. In addition, in some denominations a regular practice is to recycle pastors every two years.

How very different our churches would be if they worked together as an organism under Christ's headship. Dr. J. Wilbur Chapman in his first pastorate was visited by a layman who frankly told him, "You are not a strong preacher. In the usual order of things you will fail here, but a little group of laymen have agreed to gather every Sunday morning and pray for you." The small group grew to a thousand as God blessed their Psalm 133 spirit.[1] Failure turns to success with support and encouragement; but when even one member is missing from active duty, the strength of the whole church is weakened.

As Lutzer says, "We are soldiers in the same army, members of the same family, and stones in the same building."[2]

> If the foot shall say, Because I am not the hand I am not of the body; is it therefore not of the body? (1 Cor. 12:15).

The one with the stuttering tongue and the foggy past could be the Moses of our generation. This is not the time to conduct uniform inspections, but to be marching together under orders. William Booth recruited ex-convicts and women to the work because the elders of his denomination were too busy with their internal affairs to be about their Father's business. Booth and his army went into the streets and got the job done!

Edith Schaeffer says, "If it were up to the devil—he would subtract every one of God's people from history, and would divide all of God's people from each other, setting them at each other's throats, with hate erasing love, and occupation with lesser battles diverting their attention from the major battle of God against Satan!"[3] The church needs workers, not wrecking crews!

Abraham Lincoln's heart's desire was a minimum of hate as the end of the Civil War came into sight and the awesome tasks of reconstruction and reconciliation loomed. When a Massachusetts Senator approached him concerning Jefferson Davis, saying "Do not allow him to escape the law. He must be hanged!" Lincoln calmly replied, "Judge not that ye be not judged." The conviction that took him into the war gave him the right attitude following it: A house divided against itself cannot stand.

The spiritual war is over. We have been reconciled to God and to each other by the shedding of Blood. Now there is a mystical union between Christ and His Church. "He that is joined to the Lord is one Spirit" (1 Cor. 6:17). We are members of His body, His flesh and His bones. We do not attack God's people when they are down because Christ died to lift them up. We do not malign a child of God because he is God's child. The One he is joined to will take care of him.

Christianity has let down its breastplate, which is **Christ's** righteousness. While human integrity is crying for men to pay penance in order to make things right, divine integrity proclaims that Jesus already made it right. By cross-examining our own, we are contradicting the very message we have been commissioned to bring the world. "All have sinned, and fallen short of the glory of God" (Rom. 3:23). The wages of sin is death but the gift of God gives us what we do not deserve—a full pardon and the imputation of Christ's own righteousness. "For He hath made Him to be sin for us, Who knew no sin; that we might be made the righteousness of God in Him" (2

Cor. 5:21). All those who receive the "abundance of grace and the gift of righteousness shall reign in life by one, Jesus Christ" (Rom. 5:17).

As we hold out this gift to the world, are we living by it ourselves? When we leave the position of victory in Christ which God has given us, we have no other stand. We are defeated the moment we step down from Christ's work on the cross to compare our works in relative righteousness.

"To him that worketh not, but believeth on him that justifieth the ungodly, his faith is counted for righteousness" (Rom. 4:5). The moment we stop deriving all our righteousness from the Son, we are unrighteous in our thinking. What is the work of God which He expects from us? "This is the work of God, that ye believe on Him whom He hath sent" (John 6:29). We commit the deepest sin of all against God when we disannul Christ's fulfillment of righteousness by demanding human payment.

The Sins of the Church

The top seven sins listed in Proverbs 6:16-19 all have their origin in pride. The first listed is "a proud look." Pride lifts the Christian above his brethren while humility would esteem a brother better than oneself. "Hereby perceive we the love of God because He laid down His life for us: and we ought to lay down our lives for the brethren."

The second sin is "a lying tongue." The apostle Paul said, "Let God be true and every man a liar" in reference to those who received the oracles of God but did not believe them. The Pharisees kept the Law but when the Perfection of the Law came in the form of Jesus Christ, they would not believe. "But, when that which is perfect is come, then that which is in part shall be done away" says the great love chapter, 1 Corinthians 13. Christ is THE truth and every partial truth which falls short of the totality of Christ is a lie. To expose the sins of others is to lie against the One who bore those sins on His own body in order to put them behind His back. Hundreds and hundreds of Christians live in unresolved problems because they lie against the truth that in Christ the sin issue is settled and that in Him we are free.

The third sin that God hates is "hands that shed innocent blood." The devil, according to Jesus, was a murderer from the beginning. He assassinated God's character before the angels and murdered man's spirit by his false representation of Him in Eden's garden. The first human murder was committed in reaction to the gift of grace and the imputation of righteousness without works. If we do not accept what Christ's blood has done, we will want to shed human blood in one way or another.

The fourth sin is "an heart that deviseth wicked imaginations." Negative planning based on false information leads to the fifth sin, "feet that be swift in running to mischief." How many phone calls, gossip sessions, and board meetings have been held with the motive to destroy!

The sixth sin is being "a false witness." Testimonies which deny the truth of Calvary lead to the final sin, "sowing discord among the brethren." All breakdowns in the church start with exalting self and self's evaluations above the cross and Christ's verdict of "It is finished." "These six things doth the Lord hate: yea, seven are an abomination unto Him."

What Is Our Message?

Have we lost our spiritual focal point? The right message will give the Church the right spirit and we will forgive one another as Christ has forgiven us. The height of deception is to profess to represent Christ but then preach personal righteousness. "Not having mine own righteousness, which is of the law, but that which is through the faith of Christ, the righteousness which is of God by faith" (Phil. 3:9). Those who try to enter God's presence on the basis of their many wonderful works will find they cannot get in. Faith in Christ's blood alone impresses God. He wants the privilege of showing off the exceeding riches of His grace demonstrated by His kindness in sending Christ to pay it all. When we finally surrender the worthlessness of our own righteousness, which continually seeks to compete with His, our energies will be put to better use. How many names in the phone book have never been prayed over because we have been more concerned with promoting ourselves instead of propagating the Gospel?

The Pharisees added 2,000 rules to the Ten Commandments and still could not enter into heaven! We are either dead in Christ through the reckoning of faith or we are dead to Christ by living according to externals, whether legalistic or lascivious. Unless the Spirit of God is reigning through our faith, the Church lives in carnality. Christianity is not a quantity of rules, but a quality of life. If we walk in the newness of the Spirit of life, we will not fulfill the lusts of the flesh. His is a **Holy** Spirit that does not have to be regulated by human effort but is received in response to divine goodness. Listen to the prayer of a spiritual five-star general for the Church:

And this I pray, that your love may abound yet
more and more in knowledge and in all judgment, that ye may approve things that are
excellent; that ye may be sincere and without
offense till the day of Christ; Being filled with
the fruits of righteousness, which are by Jesus
Christ, unto the glory and praise of God (Phil.
1:9-11).

The Church is to seek every opportunity to love with
a cup running over, having a river of life flowing perpetu-
ally, intensely, and progressively from within through
the accurate knowledge of truth. We are to perfect a
capacity to express ourselves through Christ, alone.

Things that are "excellent" refer to that which has
eternal weight. "Sincere" means free from the falsehoods
of man's understanding so that we are without offense,
never preventing someone from knowing the true nature
of God. God's love is based on imputed righteousness.
We bear the fruit of it when we love according to our
standing in Him, not in response to the state of man.

God's love has no "buts" to it. If our love can dimin-
ish, then it was never really God's love. Love has no need
of a scapegoat because it has Calvary. There is peace in
that fellowship and joy in that Presence. The Church is to
take in the love of Christ and to breathe it out. Without
this love, we have no proof we are of Him. "We know that
we have passed from death unto life, because we love the
brethren. He that loveth not his brother abideth in death"
(1 John 3:14).

Just as Adam and Eve had a choice whether to obey
God by partaking of the tree of Life, or to disobey by
partaking of the tree of knowledge without Life, we also
have that choice. The false ministers who troubled the

119

Galatian church had another gospel because they preached from the wrong tree. Christ did not come to judge but to give life. We are not commissioned to know anything about anyone's flesh, but to love with a love that goes beyond knowledge. The authority of the Church is to dispense forgiveness through the grace of God!

> Down in the human heart crushed by the
>   tempter,
> Feelings lie buried that grace can restore.
> Touched by a loving heart, wakened by
>   kindness,
> Chords that are broken will vibrate once more.
> —Fanny J. Crosby

The Spirit of Gathering

Gathering is the only ministry sanctioned by Christ. "He that gathereth not with Me, scattereth abroad" (Matt. 12:30). To gather means to bring together, to reconcile, to assemble. To practice anything else is to scatter and to disperse, like throwing seed to the wind. Our ministry is to build up and to gather believers around faith in Christ.

The essence of grace is its freedom of conditions. The apostle Paul was so saturated by this grace that he desired to dispense it without receiving any financial recompense. True purity comes from being rightly related to the pure grace of God. Only the grace of God accomplishes a work in the human soul.

When we evaluate people, we send them away guilty. When we edify them, we gather them into a new identity in Christ. During His three years of public ministry, Jesus consistently gathered, always covering and redeeming what had been lost. At high noon when no one else was around to hear her sin confessed, He gathered the woman at the well. Under the cover of night he met with Nicodemus to gather under His wing this religious man who did not want the other Pharisees to know his inner need. Jesus waited until all those who condemned the woman taken in adultery had gone before He addressed her. And then He said, "Neither do I condemn thee: go, and sin no more" (John 8:9-11). He, alone, had a right to condemn her but He would not. Instead, He gathered her into the kingdom of God.

Since there are none among us who can claim perfect sinlessness, our only ministry can be that of reconciliation. We have no right to engage in a ministry of accusation, condemnation, or judgment. Any who participate in a negative ministry do not gather but scatter, elevating the opinions of self above the Word of God and the Son of God. We have the right to discern scripturally in order to restore and discipline as a local church, but never to gossip, malign, or assassinate another Christian's character. When James and John, the sons of thunder, wanted to call down fire from heaven to see "justice" done, Jesus rebuked them. "Ye know not what manner of spirit ye are of. For the Son of man is not come to destroy men's lives but to save them" (Luke 9:55,56). This is the gospel of grace. Anything else is another spirit, another gospel, and another Jesus.

The Royal Law

Christ's last visit on earth was to crooked Zacheus' house; His last trip was through Jericho to heal blind Bartimeus; His last words were "This day thou shalt be with Me in Paradise" to the thief hanging by His side. This is the real Jesus, the friend of sinners and Redeemer of the human race. Some of the greatest men in the Bible were used mightily after they had failed miserably. God does not promote because of sin, but in spite of it. David wrote his greatest psalms after his greatest sins. Jonah, after rebelling and failing God, had one of the greatest revivals in human history. Peter, fifty days after denying Christ with curses, was used to win thousands as the great preacher of Pentecost. God does not bless sin, but His blood purges completely so He is able to abundantly bless where sin once reigned.

Moses was the forgiven murderer, David the forgiven adulterer, Jacob the forgiven deceiver, Jonah... Peter... Paul... forgiven! This is the saving life which we have been called to represent. God is the Father who treats His prodigal sons as honored guests. No recitation of their failure, no public confession demanded, no probation period required. In John, chapter four, the woman who had five husbands and was living in open adultery won a city to Christ. You see, the power of love does more to destroy the power of sin than judging ever could do!

Jesus used the parable of the lost coin, the lost lamb, and the lost son to depict His heart toward the overlooked, the wandering, and the rebellious. May the Church bear His nature along with His name! "God is love" (1 John 4:16). The Pharisees made a god after their own religious imaginations. Every religious system rejects its own authors because not even they can live up to its standards. Christ came for the frail and undeserving. He promotes those who keep a grace perspective. He uses the weak to surprise the strong. Behold the Lamb! The Church is to have the Lamb's Spirit and walk in His royal law of love which fulfills every other law.

"Thou shalt love thy neighbor as thyself." This is the

majestic law, expressing the highest characteristic possible of human life. It is not a law like others which lays down specific guidelines, but is a principle of living that is motivated by Calvary's grace. As one preacher put it, the royal law of love asks the question "To whom can I be a neighbor?", rather than "Who is my neighbor?" The lawyer inside the natural mind is always justifying self on the basis of external parameters, but the royal law of love cannot be lived up to. It must be shed abroad in the heart by the Holy Spirit. When we live in the flow of this love, we operate in our royal identity according to God's intended design who "hath made us kings and priests." Instead of being slaves to petty grudges, critical opinions, jealous thoughts, and selfish motives, we reign with Him. God's love forgives and forgets the moment of becoming conscious of being sinned against.

> Ye have heard that it hath been said, Thou shalt love thy neighbor, and hate thine enemy. But I say unto you, Love your enemies, bless them that curse you, do good to them that hate you, and pray for them which despitefully use you, and persecute you; that ye may be the children of your Father which is in heaven: for He maketh His sun to rise on the evil and on the good, and sendeth rain on the just and on the unjust. For if ye love them which love you, what reward have ye? do not even the publicans the same? And if ye salute your brethren only, what do ye more than others? do not even the publicans so? Be ye therefore perfect, even as your Father which is in heaven is perfect (Matt. 5:43-48).

Even when love is grieved, it never changes. Love controls the thoughts, tongue, and behavior when the Lamb is allowed His throne. Worthy is the Lamb and outside of Him, none are worthy. Through the reckoning of the Cross, we receive His Spirit so that we can conquer through love. If Christ is truly our Master, we will wash each other's feet with forgiveness, reconciliation, and restoration. There is no reason to expose others here on earth. It serves no redemptive purpose to make judgments before the world. Everything will be tried at the appointed time at the Bema Seat Judgment of Christ. Until then, let us live by faith, redeeming the time while resting in love. Now is the time to put everything else aside and preach **Christ**!

Forget It

If you see a tall fellow ahead of the crowd,
A leader of music, marching fearless and proud,
And you know of a tale whose mere telling
    aloud
Would cause his proud head to in anguish be
    bowed,
        It's a pretty good plan to forget it.

If you know of a skeleton hidden away
In a closet, and guarded and kept from the day
In the dark; whose showing, whose sudden
    display
Would cause grief and sorrow and lifelong
    dismay
        It's a pretty good plan to forget it.

If you know of a spot in the life of a friend
(We all have spots concealed, world without
   end)
Whose touching his heartstrings would play or
   rend,
Till the shame of its showing no grieving could
   mend,
           It's a pretty good plan to forget it.

If you know of a thing that will darken the joy
Of a man or a woman, a girl or boy,
That will wipe out a smile or the least way
   annoy
A fellow, or cause any gladness to cloy
           It's a pretty good plan to forget it.
                    —Anonymous

Full Restoration

Divine love bears all things, believes all things, hopes all things, and endures all things (1 Cor. 13:7). As Christians filled with the love of God, we must take the position that no believer purposefully fails. We all have sinned. "If we say that we have no sin, we deceive ourselves, and the truth is not in us. If we confess our sins, He is faithful and just to forgive us our sins, and to cleanse us from all unrighteousness" (John 1:8,9). If God should mark iniquity, who could stand? David rejoiced that God's forgiveness washed away his sin and restored him fully before God and men: "Blessed is he whose transgression is forgiven, whose sin is covered. Blessed is the man unto whom the Lord imputeth not iniquity" (Ps. 32:1-2). Before David confessed his sin, he was under the heavy conviction of the Holy Spirit. But when David acknowledged his sin instead of hiding it, God's mercy was quick to bury it in the sea of His forgetfulness.

> Come now, and let us reason together, saith the Lord: though your sins be as scarlet, they shall be as white as snow; though they be red like crimson, they shall be as wool (Isa. 1:18).

Paul urged the congregation to forgive and comfort the man who had repented of his affair with his step-mother. They were to receive him back into fellowship immediately "lest somehow such a one be overwhelmed by excessive sorrow" (2 Cor. 2:7;NASB). The prodigal's father instantly restored his son to his former position and sense of self-worth. A kiss, not punishment, awaits the return of the backslider. Our own sins punish us in the sowing and reaping process, but God forgives and covers. He is not dealing with sins but with individuals who need to know their personal significance in His plan.

Christ was both High Priest and sacrifice. He called Mary by name before ascending to "My Father and your Father." Now, His blood on the mercy seat in the Holy of Holies makes God "Our Father" even in our darkest hour of sin and shame.

> Thou that hast slept in error's sleep
> Oh, wouldst thou wake in Heaven,
> Like Mary kneel, like Mary weep,
> "Love much," and be forgiven?
> —Thomas Moore

The love of God has removed the sin from the sinner. "As far as the east is from the west, so far hath He removed our transgressions from us"! (Ps. 103:12). Though we fall, we are not utterly cast down because of being upheld by the nail-scarred hands.

Even if the fallen believer is never restored on earth, his salvation is upheld in heaven. Saul, the first monarch of Israel, came under the influence of darkness and never recovered. But David attests to his salvation by saying "Saul and Jonathan were lovely and pleasant in their lives, and in their death they were not divided" (2 Sam. 1:23). David called him anointed even when he was not manifesting his anointing. Saul went to Paradise with his son, just as Samuel who rose from the Paradise side of Hades had prophesied: "tomorrow shalt thou and thy sons be with me." To say that Saul went to a place of torment to pay for his sins would be to say that Samuel and Jonathan went there, too.

David, on the other hand, repented of his adultery and act of murder so he was fully restored. Although his sin greatly affected others, he said "Against Thee, Thee only, have I sinned, and done this evil in Thy sight" (Ps. 51:4). The prophet Nathan was used to confront David because his sin was affecting the entire kingdom but David's repentance was before God, alone. He was not subjected to any official investigation or board of inquiry. He was not even put on probation. The sin which was exposed in private was confessed in private and God, alone, did the chastising. The baby born of his adulterous union with Bathsheba died but so complete was God's forgiveness that He chose the second child born of their love, Solomon, to reign as the next king. Hundreds of years later, God, Himself, was not ashamed to be associated with the name of the one who had failed but who had forsaken his sin, as Matthew opens his gospel with "Jesus Christ, the son of David."

Restoration of a Leader

I respect the marvelous men of God who disagree with my views on this subject. I highly honor their convictions and their fruit and I love them very much. However, nowhere in the New Testament does it say that a leader cannot be restored to his full rights of office if he has confessed and forsaken his sin. *APOKATASTASIS* is the Greek word for restoration, which means to set back in order according to original position. A pastor should be blameless in his lifestyle but he cannot be perfect because his adamic nature has not been eradicated. In Philippians 3:12, Paul said "neither am I already perfect"—it was then already quite late in his ministry. A leader has greater responsibility before God. The correction he receives on earth from God will be more rigorous than a member of the congregation who sins, and he will be more accountable at the judgment seat of Christ. A leader should submit to the organizational policy of the denomination which he embraces, but should also be fully restored according to the Scriptures. There is a higher standard of discipline for a pastor if he fails, but his restoration is not anything less than complete once he has repented. All the rights and privileges of his office, including preaching, are his to exercise because they were given to him through the unconditional gift and unchanging calling of Christ.

Abraham was not disqualified as the father of our faith when he produced Ishmael through Hagar. He was chastised and then restored to become the father of Isaac. God was not any less holy back then! Solomon sinned profusely after becoming king. But in his old age he was used to write two inspired books of Scripture. God did not relegate him to a secondary work but allowed him to continue in his original calling as His spokesman. Taking the position that a pastor cannot be fully restored after repenting from sin puts limits on the finished work of Christ, God's ability and desire to forgive, the meaning and purpose of restoration, the efficacy of Christ's priesthood, and does despite to the Spirit of Grace. Above all, it is not according to God's Word. As a leader in Romans 7:19, Paul said that he did evil. In Luke 5:6-8, Peter said, "I have sinned." Later, after denying the Lord, He was restored to his full position of leadership.

According to Matthew 5:28, mental sins are just as serious as overt ones. Should every pastor who thinks a lustful thought step down from the pulpit? If that were the case, who would be left to preach? James 2:10-13 says that to offend one point of the Law is to offend it all. The same Law which says "thou shalt not commit adultery" also says "thou shalt not covet." There are no "special" sins which require special chastisement. How can we extend unconditional forgiveness of sins to the world, but withhold it from our own? If Christ died to forgive the unsaved sinner, He will not do less for His own sons.

> He that spared not His own Son, but delivered Him up for us all, how shall He not with Him also freely give us all things? Who shall lay anything to the charge of God's elect? It is God that justifieth. Who is he that condemneth? It is Christ that died, yea rather, that is risen again, who is even at the right hand of God, who also maketh intercession for us (Rom. 8:31-34).

Let us not muzzle a preacher of the good news from partaking of his own message. He needs the grace of God, too!

The Attitude of the Onlooker

Don't sneer at the man who is down today,
Unless you have felt the blow
That caused his fall, or felt the shame
That only the fallen know.
—Anonymous

Job's friends were ready to trample him when he was down. Little did they realize that they were being tested as surely as he was! While the sins of the Mary Magdelenes and Zaccheus' of our day make headlines, God is quietly taking notes on the hearts of those who judge. God does not impute the cause of sin, the actual sin, or its effects once a sin has been confessed and forsaken. Those who require more than God does are not walking in the Light, themselves. The same Light that requires a fallen Christian to repent, requires his brothers to restore him and not tell others. Love covers the multitude of sins. The prodigal son's older brother was disturbed when his father threw a party for the repentant sibling. He wanted his brother to suffer more than he had already suffered. The elder brother spirit in the Father's house must go!

In certain circles and organizations, a pastor who sins is subjected to proceedings that come close to violating constitutional principles. These legalists should consider a ban on portions of Scripture such as the Psalms, Ecclesiastes and Song of Solomon which were written after periods of backsliding. If Abraham or Jacob were alive today, they would say: "Abraham disqualified himself. I'm afraid he can't be considered for the job," or "Jacob? I can't respect him. He was a cheat!" Though they say they forgive, they never forget when someone fails. This interpretation of restoration is partial and conditional, clearly violating the very foundation of the new covenant. In her little book "*If*", Amy Carmichael zeros in on Christian hypocrisy. She writes:

> If I cast up a confessed, repented, and forsaken sin against another, and allow my remembrance of that sin to color my thinking and feed my suspicions, then I know nothing of Calvary love.

And again,

> If I say, Yes, I forgive, but I cannot forget, as though the God, who twice a day washes all the sands on all the shores of all the world, could not wash such memories from my mind, then I know nothing of Calvary love.

No License For Sin

All God's children should hate sin. One brief look from the Lord caused backslidden Peter to weep bitter tears. The Apostle probably never forgot that look. Every time we sin, we hurt Christ and our own souls. Living in sin is not fun and games. God is in control of the situation, no matter how things appear. The Christian who does not repent loses the joy and privileges of daily fellowship with the Lord. He comes under the discipline of his Heavenly Father whose chastening is progressive, and grows in intensity for as long as he refuses to repent. David wrote in Psalm 118:18, "The Lord hath chastened me sore: but he hath not given me over unto death." Apparently, the chastening was so intense that David literally feared for his life. The year that David waited before confessing his sin with Bathsheba was not an enjoyable one for the King of Israel.

The Lord does not discipline in anger. He disciplines in mercy and love because He desires fellowship with the believer. His purpose is always restoration and reconciliation. In all of His dealings with us, He has our best interests in mind. He wants us to be happy, productive and mature, progressively becoming conformed to the image of His Son.

TEN

BEAUTY FOR ASHES

> To comfort all who mourn, ... Giving them a garland instead of ashes, the oil of gladness instead of mourning, the mantle of praise instead of a spirit of fainting. So they will be called oaks of righteousness, the planting of the Lord, that He might be glorified (Isa. 61:2,3; NASB).

This was Christ's mission. His sacrifice turned our sins into ashes which leave no evidence of what has been burned. All that may be discerned from ashes is that there was an offering made, accepted, and utterly consumed.

An untold number of beautiful success stories have risen out of the ashes. I received a moving letter from a pastor who listens to my radio program. Many years ago, he committed adultery with a woman in his congregation. She was the first to repent and then begged him to repent as well, which he did. His church is now prospering because this woman saved the day by handling the sin divine-style. Instead of setting herself up as the "victim" who decides to tell all in a fit of "truth," she confessed her sin only to God and to the person involved. The illicit relationship was totally cut off but she stayed in the church and continues to serve to this day under the pastor's wife who does not know what had happened. This is the integrity spoken of in Proverbs 17:9:

> He that covereth a transgression seeketh love:
> But he that repeateth a matter separateth very
> friends.

While some in the Church are in the detecting business, God is in the protecting business! "It is the glory of God to conceal a thing: but the honor of kings is to search out a matter" (Prov. 25:2). This woman had the spirit of a Deborah and saved the situation under Christ's headship. Love always does that which would reconcile, save, and influence for good. Knowledge puffs up one's sense of self-importance, but love edifies everyone concerned. That woman saved the pastor's marriage, family, pastorate, and church, as well as his unrealized potential. How much better than what has been happening wholesale these days as men's sins are being broadcast over the network so that those involved have no future.

One young couple had only been married two and a half years when the husband committed adultery. He repented and returned to the Lord very shortly after, but the woman with whom he had relations had already conceived. She confronted his wife with the story. In tears, the hurting wife sought God's mind. The other woman did not want the child, so the wife decided to take the child as her own. Years have passed and no one knows that the child is not hers. She and her husband have kept the secret between themselves. The wife never once brought it up to use it as an accusation against him in difficult times. The husband has thanked her thousands of times over through his heartfelt love and appreciation. Their marriage is a trophy of grace built on the foundation of forgiveness. The valley of weeping became a door of hope because the God of all grace turned the curse into a blessing.

In the early days of my first pastorate, two people in my ministry became involved with each other. No one around them knew of the affair. One morning while I was doing a radio broadcast, the Spirit of God revealed it to me. The tears flowed down my cheeks. We had to put a taped message on because my heart was breaking and I could not continue the broadcast. I had them both come into my office where they confessed to the affair. The woman, especially, was very broken and desirous of letting Christ be her complete victory. During the ensuing days as she sought the Lord for spiritual restoration, God gave me a song to encourage her heart:

He woke me in the morning, I thought of His
    love,
He opened my ear with His heavenly dove.
The sunrise was splendor, the sky was so blue,
Fresh dew on the grass, white clouds pure and
    true.

God gave me a new day, tears came from my
    eyes,
I can go on now with no grief or sighs,
Thank you, my Father, I'm refreshed in my
    soul,
My precious Lord Jesus has made me whole.

Even me, even me, He has made me whole,
Jesus, my Lord had transformed my soul.
Oh, what a difference this Saviour in me,
Christ Jesus, my Lord, has set me free!

Unfortunately, this story does not have a happy ending. She told her husband about the relationship and he could not forgive her. He put her on trial for the next year of their marriage, not even wanting to kiss her. His coldness and accusations were too much for her to bear in her already broken state. She went back to the arms of the other man and her marriage ended in divorce. Her husband reinforced her poor self-image and guilt until she gave up on herself. But, though her heart condemned her, God's love was greater than her heart. God had forgiven and forgotten her sin but her husband had not. He failed the grace of God in his hour of opportunity. "The Lord upholdeth all that fall, and raiseth up all those that be bowed down" (Ps. 145:14). As members of a fallen race, this is the kind of love we need in order to make it.

Grace upon Grace

God's grace is the only answer for the human condition. Lewis Sperry Chafer, the great theologian, said that grace finds its greatest triumph when we are the most helpless. Grace cannot be less for the worst, or better for the best because it is not given on the basis of merit or withdrawn for demerit. Grace is ontological—the quality of God's own being which pervades all of His attributes. God was grace before there ever was a creation to receive its benefits. Sin does not stop grace; only the rejection of grace by the free will can inhibit it. The Pharisees revered outward morality, self-righteousness, the distinctions of rank, and even the Scriptures, but they did not love who God was—GRACE! Christ, Himself, authors and finishes our faith. Grace gives us a place in the plan of God and maintains our place in that plan. Like Abraham, like Jacob, like Moses, like Peter, like Paul we cannot sin our way out of His plan of grace. Grace will not accept the excuses of our demerits. "Whither shall I flee from Thy Presence? If I ascend up into heaven, Thou art there: if I make my bed in hell, behold Thou art there" (Ps. 139:7-8). The soul that realizes it cannot flee from God's love ultimately submits to it!

"I am persuaded," Paul said. The Spirit finally convinced him that nothing could separate him from God's love. Knowing this quality of grace so satisfies the heart that it does not want to sin or be separated from its fellowship. When grace is on the throne, we are motivated to pray, to love, and to bring others to Christ. The only possible premise for human existence is grace. Common grace provides us with health, home, and happiness. Calvary's grace gives us heaven. Greater grace makes us progressively more like Jesus right here in time. Grace takes man from the cradle to the grave, perfecting him in love.

> For whom He did foreknow, He also did predestinate to be conformed to the image of His Son, that He might be the first born among many brethren. Moreover whom He did predestinate, them He also called: and whom He called, them He also justified: and whom He justified, them He also glorified (Rom. 8:29-30).

God is waiting to be gracious. We have not begun to tap His inexhaustible supply. Those who know this kind of a God are able to do great exploits, but those who think they serve a hard Taskmaster bury their talents and never use them. A. W. Tozer noted that the God we worship is the foundation of the whole building. Every heresy can be traced back to some imperfect thought about God. Our God is the One who will not break the bruised reed or quench the smoking flax. The flickering light will not be put out. Those who are broken will become instruments of righteousness in His hands. As we grow in knowing what God is like, His nature is worked in so that we become patient, longsuffering, hoping and loving to the end as He does. Moses cried out to this God, "That I may know Thee!", and again, "Show me Thy glory!" Paul, having served Christ many years, had one burning desire: "That I may know Him!"

Deeper dimensions of fellowship await those who do not manufacture a manageable god on their own terms, but seek to really know the God of all grace. We look to Jesus, knowing that to see Him and His compassion is to see the Father. "For God, who commanded the light to shine out of darkness, hath shined in our hearts, to give the light of the knowledge of the glory of God in the face of Jesus Christ" (2 Cor. 4:6). This is what it is all about—to know the true God and the One whom He has sent. Gracious promises have been given to draw us into His Presence. We will not give up on ourselves or others if we truly know that it is all grace.

Experiencing This Reality

An understanding of the finished work of Christ cannot be grasped overnight. Hudson Taylor struggled with Galatians 2:20 and Romans 6:6 for fifteen years. Intellectually, he comprehended co-crucifixion and his new identity, but not until the Spirit of God made it alive to his soul did he have the faith to experience it. Watchman Nee pondered Colossians 3:3 for ten years before the Spirit imparted its meaning to his spirit. The eternal being inside of every true Christian is not who we were in childhood, adolescence or even adulthood. The real "I" is in Christ, in the incorruptible seed received at the moment of the new birth. The Spirit cries out "Come hither!" He is calling us to come up to an ascended viewpoint where we can see spiritual reality.

Calvary is a real place offering a real end and a real beginning. Sixty-two percent of men and women released from prison end up back there. How we love our prisons! Abraham was called out of Ur to adventure with God into a new land. Christ stands at the door and knocks. He says to the prisoner locked behind the walls of memory and self-consciousness: "Rise up, my love, my fair one, and come away. For, lo, the winter is past, the rain is over and gone" (Song of Sol. 2:10-11). We seek a city whose builder and maker is **God**. Man-made religion is the system which killed the prophets and crucified the Saviour. Christ came to destroy, not the Law, but the system of works which usurps His Personhood of grace and which elevates ecclesiastical ego while the world goes to hell. Jesus died outside the camp of the religious stronghold of His day. "Let us go forth therefore unto Him without the camp, bearing His reproach" (Heb. 13:13). Outside an external exercise and human priesthood, we find the experience of eternal life. "Another priest arises according to the likeness of Melchizedek, who has become such not on the basis of a law of physical requirement, but according to the power of an indestructible life" (Heb. 7:15,16; NASB).

We are like the two disciples on the road to Emmaus. The crucifixion, resurrection, and ascension had all occurred but they were not alive to finished work reality. Yes, they had received Christ's teaching but it seemed useless in their situation. Christ was dead to them. Then, like Jacob waking out of his sleep and crying, "The Lord is in this place and I knew it not," their eyes were opened to see the Living Lord. Immanuel, God with us, is right here ready to explode our experience with love, forgiveness, mercy, power, and grace!

Beyond Time

Jesus said, "My kingdom is not of this world" (John 18:36). The bride in Solomon's song is described as a garden enclosed, a spring shut up, a fountain sealed. Sealed by the Holy Spirit, every child of God has an identity beyond time, beyond experience, hidden in the nature of God. Underneath are the everlasting arms. Christ is under the bottom. So when we fall in time, He is still able to keep us from falling and to present us faultless before His Presence with exceeding joy. Because all God's promises ever stand, we stand before Him blameless and in love. We can never fall out of the Father's hand because He is greater than all. God looks beyond this world into the next and asks us to set our sights there, too.

In the midst of his struggle with knowledge and sin, Paul cried out "O wretched man that I am! Who shall deliver me from the body of this death?" But in the next breath, he cried, "I thank God through Jesus Christ!" His will to do good only exacerbated evil within. When he found grace in the midst of his inadequacy, he was released by spiritual life. He realized that mercy was covering him while he worked out his faith in a process and learned how to let God be God within him. The process is private and before God, not for the eyes of this world to see.

When David went on a spiritual vacation and fell into sin, it not only hurt the Lord, but himself, too. He became like a wild bull caught in the net of lust and broken communion. He experienced a year of inner silence and heartache. The little shepherd boy lost his relationship with God, but only heaven knew. He had gotten proud as king and had grown lax with inner disciplines. His sin found him out and the sword came back on his own household, but he died with the epitaph: "David did that which was right in the eyes of the Lord, and turned not aside from any thing that He commanded him all the days of his life." (The clause in 1 Kings 15:5 qualifying God's unequivocal commendation "save only in the matter of Uriah" was added later by the translators, not being in the original.)

David's life was a finished work—enclosed, shut up and sealed in the mind of God. "Thou art all fair, my love; there is no spot in thee" (Song of Sol. 4:7). The trials and valleys David went through led to the formation of the mature believer who wrote Psalm Twenty-three. He found his identity not in his ups and downs but in God, Himself. When he lost everything in the Absalom revolution, he did not want. Green pastures and still waters characterized his spiritual walk in the midst of outward chaos and strife. It is not who we are or what we do, but who we are becoming in spiritual reality. Now is not the time that the sons of God will be made completely manifest to the natural eye. Who we are is still hid with Christ in God.

A New Name

A name signifies representation. After Jacob wrestled with the angel, he received a new name. Jacob, the usurper, became Israel, a prince with God. Rachel originally named Benjamin "Benoni," meaning "son of my sorrow." Adam is the name given to us by our first parents, representing our fallen nature. Benjamin's father changed his name and so has our Father in heaven! "Put on the new man" means to take on a new nature. In the early church, "Christian" was a brand new name given to those who walked in Christ's way. In the Book of Revelation, a new name was written on the foreheads of those who followed the Lamb wherever He went. The Bible is filled with name changes. Abram became Abraham, Jabez became Jarvis, Simon became Peter, Saul became Paul, and Joses became Barnabas through the transformational process of faith. God's changing power turned a murderer into the meekest man of the earth—Moses. Our weakest area can become the strongest because we have a new name and are growing in the potential of our new identity. "Wherefore, henceforth know we no man after the flesh" (2 Cor. 5:16). A new name is written down in glory and every believer can say "It is mine!"

A biography, ideally, is the objective account of a person's life. Biographies may or may not line up with the autobiography of the subject. God has written our biographies in the Bible. Our lives in Christ begin with an obituary with only a gravestone marking where the old life met its end in the death and burial of Christ. Now, every day we are writing an autobiography which should line up with the biography in God's library. We will be judged by its accordance with the manifest facts! There is life after death, and we are living it!

The priests of the old covenant offered animal sacrifices which were not able to purge the conscience from the consciousness of sin. The priests could not abide in God's presence in the Holy of Holies, but served Him from the middle court. Christians today serve God with secret guilt and emotional defilement because they do not realize that the veil of the flesh has been rent and they can live boldly in their seated position with Christ. A new name means no more consciousness of sin! There is nothing between us and the Lord. Instead of dwelling on our problems, we need to believe that they have been resolved at the cross. The debt of sin has not just been crossed out; it has been blotted out leaving no record of the amount that was wiped away.

Only having a single eye on grace can develop the human potential. Our goal is not to live up to the demands of the law but to live up to our potential in Christ. To be all I can be is the issue by using the provision God has given in Jesus Christ to the fullest. Making comparisons defeats the unique purpose of the individual believer. Each is a member in particular. The woman in Mark 14 did what she could, and her deed was not only accepted but eternally recorded. The godly mother will receive as many rewards as the faithful preacher if her service was unto the Lord in response to His death, burial and resurrection. In the story of the talents, the one not rightly related to the Master's love and grace buried what he had been given. He never did anything with what he had because he had the wrong concept of the One who gave it. Our only competition is with our own potential. As we utilize grace, we grow in our capacity to represent the Giver.

A Ministry of Reconciliation

And above all things have fervent charity among yourselves: for charity shall cover the multitude of sins. As every man hath received the gift, even so minister the same, one to another, as good stewards of the manifold grace of God (1 Peter 4:8,10).

Jesus, after washing the dung stains from the disciples' feet, said, "A new commandment I give unto you, That ye love one another; as I have loved you, that ye also love one another. By this shall all men know that ye are My disciples, if ye have love one to another" (John 13:34-35). No servant had been there to wash their feet in the upper room. (Peter probably thought it would be a good job for Andrew to do, who had no leadership gifts!) But it did not occur to any of them to take on the task themselves. How right Jesus was when He said "Whither I go, thou canst not follow Me now; but thou shalt follow Me afterwards." They had no capacity to lay down their lives for each other because they had not yet been filled with the Spirit of the Cross-Bearer.

It is the Spirit of the living God who causes a man to cry: "Oh that my head were waters, and mine eyes a fountain of tears, that I might weep day and night for the slain of the daughter of my people!" (Jer. 9:1). Jeremiah, anointed of the Holy Spirit, preached without compromise, but he also wept. The weeping prophet could not separate himself from his people's pain. "For the hurt of the daughter of my people am I hurt." To this one who so identified with these hurts did God reveal His heart toward men: "For I know the thoughts that I think toward you, saith the Lord, thoughts of peace and not of evil, to give you an expected end" (Jer. 29:11). Today, men and women are in need of these healing thoughts. In compassion, we are to "weep with them that weep," washing the feet that have failed with our tears and the cleansing message of God's forgiveness.

In the story of the good neighbor, a hated Samaritan stooped down and had compassion on a man who despised him. In John's Gospel, they called Jesus a Samaritan as a term of derision. This rejected Samaritan bent low to minister to His enemies. "God was in Christ, reconciling the world unto Himself, not imputing their trespasses unto them: and hath committed unto us the word of reconciliation" (2 Cor. 5:19).

A little eight-year-old girl in New England had been the victim of a broken home. She moved in with her grandmother while her parents went their separate ways living in alcoholism and immorality. The girl attended a local Sunday school and found comfort in her faith in Jesus. One day, this little girl was hit by a car and taken to intensive care. When she came back to consciousness, she asked for her mom and dad. They both came and sat, one on each side of the bed, holding her hands. She looked at her father and said, "Daddy, I love you even though you drink and get mad at Mommy." Then she lovingly looked at her mother and said, "Mommy, I'm asking Jesus to put you and Daddy back together." She lived for another 48 hours and then went to be with Jesus. Her heartbroken parents were reconciled and started to search for an answer to their grief and terrible sense of failure. Through their daughter's church they heard the Gospel and wholeheartedly gave their lives to Christ. Tragic as it was, the story of this little girl illustrates the great ministry of reconciliation given to all believers.

Forgiveness reconciled Joseph to his brothers, and reconciled his brothers to God's plan. When Joseph met with them, he cleared the room of everyone else because the issue was a family matter. It was not to be broadcast among the household of Pharaoh and throughout Egypt. "And Joseph said unto his brethren, Come near to me, I pray you. And they came near. And he said, I am Joseph your brother, whom ye sold into Egypt. Now therefore be not grieved, nor angry with yourselves, that ye sold me hither: for God did send me before you to preserve life" (Gen. 45:3-5).

Jesus Christ, our Joseph whom we delivered up to death, seeks only to be reconciled to those for whom He died. One day, His beautiful feet will descend upon the Mount of Olives to make all things right externally as He already has internally. Will we hear from Him, "Well done, thou good and faithful servant"? Will He thank us for extending His life and love, seeking nothing in return but the joy of seeing lives mended and restored? Or, instead of the gold of pure faith, the silver of redemptive words, and the precious stones of the Holy Spirit's fruit in our lives, will we have only the wood, hay and stubble that comes from tending Adam's small plot? Will we have welcomed many into the kingdom of God through the glorious Gospel, or will we have kept many from entering in by making the demands greater than God, Himself exacts?

In the last fifty years, Islam has increased 500%, Hinduism 116%, Buddhism 65%, but Christianity only 47%. Could the reason be that Christ and His love is no longer the central figure and force undergirding our message?

The Law says: "Measure up or die!" Jesus Christ

measured up and died. He is our righteousness. We do not have to measure up but we need to be reduced. The stones in the temple in Jerusalem were said to be hewn underground until they were five-foot square, signifying grace on every side. The habitation of God must be built on the foundation of grace, with Christ as the chief cornerstone. As lively stones in His house, the members of the Church are to open their hearts and beat down the gates of hell with the message of love. We only have a little time.

> We sow in the darkness only;
>   but the Reaper shall reap in light;
> And the day of His perfect glory
>   shall tell of the deeds of the night.
>   —Alfred J. Waterhouse

My Hope Is Built

My hope is built on nothing less
Than Jesus' blood and righteousness;
I dare not trust the sweetest frame,
But wholly lean on Jesus' name.

His oath, His covenant, His blood
Support me in the whelming flood;
When all around my soul gives way,
He then is all my hope and stay.

When He shall come with trumpet sound,
Oh, may I then in Him be found;
Dressed in His righteousness alone,
Faultless to stand before the throne.
　　　—Words of the hymn written
　　　　by Edward Mote

References

Chapter 2
1. Walter B. Knight, *Knight's Master Book of New Illustrations*, Wm. B. Eerdmans Publishing Co.
2. Lewis Sperry Chafer, *Grace*, Academic Books, Zondervan Publ. House

Chapter 4
1. Miles J. Stanford, *The Green Letters*, Zondervan Publishing Co.

Chapter 5
1. Richard Crashaw, *Christ's Victory*
2. George McDonald, From the poem, *The Woman Who Came Behind Him In The Crowd*

Chapter 6
1. Florence White Willett, *Reflections*, From *The Disciplines of Life*, V. Raymond Edman, Scripture Press Foundation

Chapter 7
1. Montgomery,*The Contrite Heart*, from *Poems For Sunshine and Shadow*, Good News Broadcasting Assoc.

Chapter 8
1. Walter B. Knight, *Knight's Master Book of New Illustrations*, Wm. B. Eerdmans Publishing Co.
2. Erwin W. Lutzer,*When A Good Man Falls*, Scripture Press Publ. Inc.
3. David G. Bromley, Introduction to *Strange Gods*

Chapter 9
1. Walter B. Knight, *Knight's Master Book of New Illustrations*, Wm. B. Erdmans Publishing Co.
2. Erwin W. Lutzer, *When A Good Man Falls*, Scripture Press Publ. Inc.
3. Edith Schaeffer, *The Tapestry*, Word Books

APPENDIX

For your study, the following are Scripture verses used in the text:

Chapter 1

Genesis 3:6	Genesis 9:21
Genesis 12:13, 20:2	Genesis 16:2
2 Samuel 11	Luke 22:57-60
Exodus 2:12	Acts 7:58, 9:1
Romans 7:18	Psalm 51:5
1 Kings 18:42-45	

Chapter 2

Psalm 139:4	Romans 5:18, 11:32
Exodus 32	John 15:4
2 Corinthians 5:14	Proverbs 3:7
Hebrews 11:6	2 Corinthians 2:14
Ephesians 1:4	1 John 1:8
Ephesians 2:6	Hebrews 2:8
1 Corinthians 15:56	John 14:6
2 Peter 1:4	Matthew 7:1-2
Matthew 9:17	Matthew 9:16
Romans 5:21	Hebrews 10:17-23
Hebrews 10:26-29	Hebrews 12:15
Hebrews 4:3	Hebrews 10:29
Hebrews 10:14	Hebrews 9:22
Hebrews 10:28-31	Ephesians 5:25
1 Corinthians 3:12	Zechariah 4:6-7
Micah 7:5-10	Job 28:3
1 Samuel 30	Romans 5:3-4
Ecclesiastes 4:9-10	Judges 16:19-30
Deuteronomy 34:8	Joshua 1:2
Luke 15:11-32	Genesis 4:7

Jonah 3:1
1 Peter 1:18-19
Psalm 138:8
Exodus 28:17-30
Revelation 12:11

John 20:24-27
Hebrews 12:24
Philippians 1:6
Isaiah 49:16
Romans 10:4, 5:17

Chapter 3

2 Corinthians 12:9
Ephesians 1:6, 2:7
Ephesians 1:18-19
Titus 2:11
Genesis 3:7
Mark 14:50
John 21:16
Genesis 22
2 Samuel 18
1 Kings 20:28

Genesis 3:5
Romans 5:8
Matthew 22:13
Psalm 18:35
Song of Solomon 2:10
Genesis 48:10-22, 49
Luke 7:44
2 Samuel 15
1 Kings 19:8

Chapter 4

Romans 10:4
Romans 7:15-20
Matthew 7:1
John 8:3
Ephesians 6:12
Genesis 38

Genesis 2:17
Matthew 23:27
1 John 1:10
Matthew 5:14
2 Samuel 12

Chapter 5

Genesis 3:15
Luke 22
1 Peter 3:19
Ephesians 1:3
Hebrews 6:13
1 Peter 5:8
2 Corinthians 5:20

Matthew 16:23
John 19:30
Hebrews 9:12, 24
Colossians 1:13
Matthew 16:16-19
Galatians 5:1
John 8:44

1 Corinthians 5:6-8
2 Peter 5:5
John 10:3
Matthew 10:30
Job 16:18
John 4:32
1 Peter 4:10

Genesis 50:19
John 13:35
John 10:3
Psalm 56:8
Luke 19:41
2 Corinthians 5:20

Chapter 6

1 Corinthians 1:30
Romans 1:7
1 John 3:2
John 1:14
2 Peter 1:4
Galatians 4:1-9
1 Corinthians 15:10
Romans 1:17
Romans 7:3
1 John 3:20
Matthew 17:1-20
Job 5:7
Joshua 3:17
2 Corinthians 4:7

Colossians 1:13
1 Thessalonians 3:12, 5:23
2 Peter 3:18
Romans 12:2
1 Corinthians 8:1-3
Hebrews 4:10
1 Peter 1:23
2 Corinthians 3:18
Hebrews 4:11
Job 23:10, 12
2 Peter 1:19
1 Peter 1:3
Hebrews 2:10

Chapter 7

Romans 8:14
Hebrews 4:2
Hebrews 4:12
2 Timothy 2:15
Acts 26:20
2 Corinthians 7:8
Hebrews 12:1-2
1 Corinthians 14:27-40
2 Timothy 4:2

James 4:11
Romans 10:17
Ephesians 4:11
Hebrews 12:16-17
Luke 5:8
Philippians 2:12-13
Luke 19:8
2 Corinthians 10:8
Genesis 3:16

1 Corinthians 11:10
2 Corinthians 2:6-8
Acts 5
Romans 14:3, 4
1 Corinthians 10:29
Genesis 9:20-27
Acts 9:4

Ephesians 5:16
1 Corinthians 5:11
1 Corinthians 4:1-6
Romans 14:22
2 Samuel 1:20
Judges 5:23

Chapter 9

1 Corinthians 9:3, 11:28
Matthew 12:25
Philippians 2:3
Romans 3:4
Genesis 4
Matthew 7:22
Galatians 1:6-8, 5:16
2 Corinthians 5:14-19
John 3, 4
Luke 19
Luke 15, 23:43
John 1:36
Romans 5:5
1 Corinthians 4:5
Micah 7:19
Psalm 37:24
James 3:1
1 Peter 4:10

2 Corinthians 13:5
Ephesians 5:20
1 John 3:16
John 8:44
John 19:30
Ephesians 2:7
John 12:47
1 Corinthians 9:18
2 Corinthians 11:3-4
Mark 10:46
1 Corinthians 1:27
Luke 10:29
Revelation 1:6, 5:12
Psalm 130:3
John 20:17
1 Samuel 26:9, 28:20
Romans 11:29
Luke 22:61-62

Chapter 10

1 Corinthians 8:1
Hebrews 12:2
Hebrews 4:16
2 Corinthians 5:14
Daniel 11:32

Hosea 2:15
Romans 8:38
1 John 3:16
Isaiah 30:18
Matthew 25:24-25

Isaiah 42:3
Philippians 3:10
Revelation 21:9-10, 3:20
Genesis 28:16
Song of Solomon 4:12
Deuteronomy 33:27
Ephesians 1:4
Colossians 3:1
Isaiah 51:20
Romans 8:19
Genesis 32:28, 35:18
Revelation 14:1-4
Psalm 51:9
1 Corinthians 12:27
Genesis 45
1 Corinthians 1:30
1 Peter 4:10

Exodus 3:13, 18
John 14:9, 17:3
Hebrews 11:10
Luke 24:31
Ephesians 1:13
Jude 24
John 10:29
Romans 7:25
1 John 3:2
Colossians 3:3
Ephesians 4:24
Hebrews 9:13-14, 10:2, 22
Isaiah 43:25, 44:22
Matthew 25:24
Matthew 23:13
1 Kings 6:7